Explore Rome 33

Worth a Trip

Survival Guide 173

Special Features

COVID-19

We have re-checked every business in this book to ensure that it is still open after the COVID-19 outbreak. However, the economic and social impacts of COVID-19 will continue to be felt long after the outbreak has been contained, and many businesses, services and events referenced in this guide may experience ongoing restrictions. Some businesses may be temporarily closed, have changed their opening hours and services, or require bookings; some unfortunately could have closed permanently. We suggest you check with venues before visiting for the latest information.

Rome's Top Experiences

Tour the Colosseum (p36).

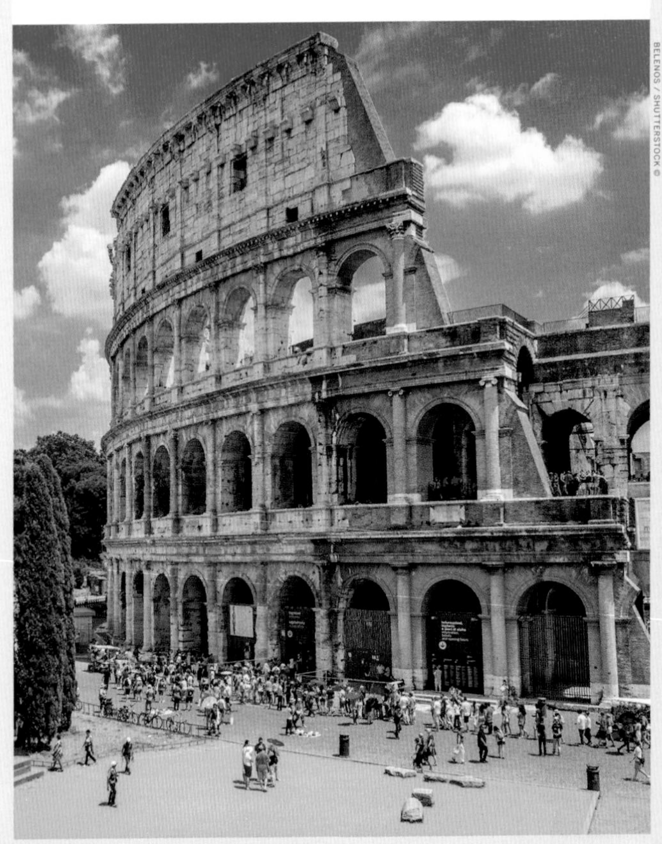

BELENOS / SHUTTERSTOCK ©

MISTERVLAD / SHUTTERSTOCK ©

Discover a masterpiece at the Vatican Museums (p74).

TTSTUDIO / SHUTTERSTOCK ©

Gaze in wonder at the Pantheon (p54).

EVGENII IAROSHEVSKII / SHUTTERSTOCK ©

Admire the artworks at Museo e Galleria Borghese (p112).

Marvel at St Peter's Basilica (p80).

EVGENII IAROSHEVSKII / SHUTTERSTOCK ©

SUTTIPONG SUTIRATANACHAI / GETTY IMAGES ©

Wander through the Roman Forum (p40).

Toss a coin in the Trevi Fountain (p94).

NINELLE / SHUTTERSTOCK ©

JANNIS TOBIAS WERNER / SHUTTERSTOCK ©

Traverse the Via Appia Antica (p154).

Explore Basilica di San Giovanni in Laterano (p134).

LEFTERIS PAPAULAKIS / SHUTTERSTOCK ©

ANNA PAKUTINA / SHUTTERSTOCK ©

Peruse the treasures of Palazzo Massimo alle Terme (p118).

Climb the Spanish Steps and explore Piazza di Spagna (p96).

S.BORISOV / SHUTTERSTOCK ©

ELENA ODAREEVA / SHUTTERSTOCK ©

Visit Basilica di Santa Maria in Trastevere (p160).

Dining Out

This is a city that lives to eat. Food feeds the Roman soul, and a social occasion would be nothing without it. Over recent decades the restaurant scene has become increasingly sophisticated, but traditional no-frills trattorias still provide Rome's most memorable gastronomic experiences.

Roman Trattorias

The bedrock of the Roman food scene has long been the family-run trattorias that pepper the city's streets and piazzas. These simple eateries, often with rickety wooden tables and *nonna* (grandma) at the stove, have been feeding visitors for centuries and are still the best bet for no-nonsense Roman dishes such as *amatriciana* (a tomato sauce flavoured with *guanciale* – cured pig's cheek – and served with pasta, typically thick spaghetti called *bucatini*) or *carbonara* (*guanciale*, egg and salty *pecorino romano* cheese paired with spaghetti or rigatoni pasta tubes).

Street Food

Street food is hugely popular in Rome and recent years have seen a trend for gourmet fast food sweep the city. Alongside *pizza al taglio* (sliced pizza) joints and gelaterie, you'll find numerous places serving classic snacks such as *supplì* (fried rice balls with various fillings) and *fritti* (fried foods) with a modern twist.

Best Sliced Pizza

Bonci Pizzarium Pizza slices created by the master, Gabriele Bonci. (p89)

Forno Roscioli Thin and crispy, this is some of the best pizza rossa (with tomato) in Rome, if not the world. (p65)

La Renella Historic bakery known for its bread, biscuits and pizza slices. (p167)

Antico Forno Urbani Kosher bakery in the Ghetto with incredible pizza bianca (with olive oil and rosemary). (p65)

TANIA VOLOBUEVA / GETTY IMAGES ©

Best Gelato

Fatamorgana Rome's finest artisanal flavours, now in multiple central locations. (p104)

Gelateria del Teatro Around 40 choices of delicious ice cream, all made on site. (p66)

Gelateria Dei Gracchi A taste of heaven in several locations across Rome. (p89)

Fior di Luna Great artisan ice cream in Trastevere. (p167)

Best Traditional Roman

Flavio al Velavevodetto Classic *cucina romana* in a popular neighbourhood trattoria. (p145)

Da Enzo Hugely popular Trastevere address, known for quality sourced ingredients. (p168)

Hostaria Romana A model trattoria good for the Roman staples. (p105)

Best Modern Roman

L'Arcangelo Updated takes on classic Roman dishes at this Prati favourite. (p90)

Pianostrada Modern Roman dining with a strong emphasis on vegetables. (p66)

La Ciambella Set over the ancient Terme di Agrippa, but the cuisine is unabashedly modern. (p67)

Salumeria Roscioli Deli-restaurant serving traditional food with a contemporary sensibility. (p67)

Top Tips

- In restaurants, it's standard practice to be given bread and charged for it whether you eat it or not.
- Tipping: round the bill up or leave a euro or two in pizzerias/trattorias; five to 10% is fine in smarter restaurants.

Bar Open

There's simply no city with better backdrops for a coffee or drink than Rome: you can sip espresso in historic cafes, claim piazza seating for an aperitivo or wander from wine bar to restaurant to late-night drinking den, getting happily lost down picturesque cobbled streets in the process.

Where to Drink

Options range from traditional cafes, seemingly unchanged in centuries, to old-school *enoteche* (wine bars), craft beer pubs, and chic lounge bars serving *aperitivi* to the glitterati. The hottest drinking trend right now is for expertly-mixed cocktails served in backroom speakeasies. Some of these hidden bars require patrons to pay a small membership fee, usually around €5. Many long-standing cocktail bars also double as laid-back cafes by day – Trastevere has plenty of examples.

Clubbing

Rome's clubbing action, largely centred on Ostiense and Testaccio, caters to most tastes with DJs playing everything from lounge and jazz to dancehall and hip-hop. Clubs tend to get busy after midnight, or even after 2am, and while admission is sometimes free, drinks are expensive.

Best Cafes

Sciascia Caffè Delicious coffee in an elegant interior. (p90)

Caffè Sant'Eustachio Historic *centro storico* (historic centre) cafe serving exceptional coffee. (p68)

La Bottega del Caffè Terrace seating overlooking Monti's prettiest piazza; great coffee, too. (p128)

Barnum Cafe Laid-back Friends-style cafe with shabby-chic furniture and good coffee. (p69)

Antico Caffè Greco Located near the Spanish Steps, this 1760 charmer is Rome's oldest cafe. (p107)

Best Wine Bars

Rimessa Roscioli Gourmet wine bar offering wine tastings and delicious food. (p59)

Wine Concept Run by expert sommeliers, with an

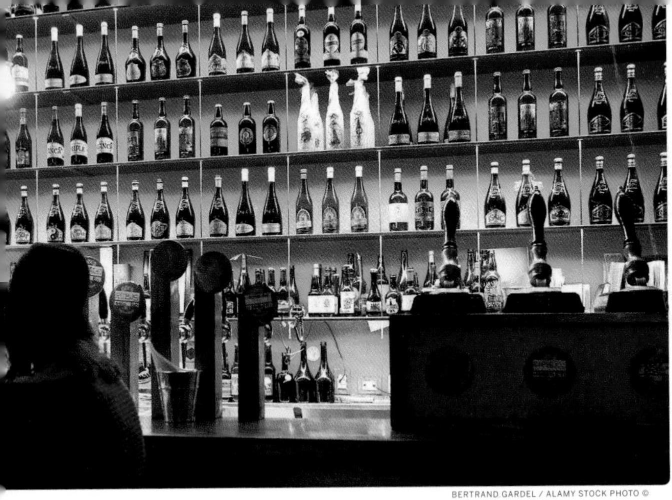

extensive list of Italian regional labels and European vintages. (p140)

Ai Tre Scalini Buzzing *enoteca* that feels as convivial as a pub. (p127)

Best Aperitivo

Freni e Frizioni Perennially cool bar with lavish nightly buffet of snacks. (p163)

Doppiozeroo Popular Ostiense address with impressive buffet choice. (p153)

Rec 23 Hip New York–inspired venue offering Testaccio's best *aperitivi*. (p151)

Lettere Caffè The *aperitivo* spread at this inclusive Trastevere cafe is all-vegetarian. (p170)

Best Speakeasies

Blackmarket Hall Monti speakeasy with cosy corners and weekend jazz sets. (p127)

Club Derrière At the rear (get it?) of a trattoria, with top-notch cocktails. (p70)

Keyhole Prohibition-era decor and large menu of craft cocktails. (p169)

Best Beer

Bar San Calisto Linger over cheep beer at this popular Trastevere hang-out. (p169)

Ma Che Siete Venuti a Fà Pint-sized bar crammed with real-ale choices. (p170)

Open Baladin More than 40 beers on tap and up to 100 bottled brews. (pictured; p68)

Artisan Craft beers from Italy and overseas. (p131)

Top Tip

Romans tend to dress up to go out, especially in the smarter clubs and bars in the *centro storico* (historic centre) and Testaccio. Over in Pigneto and San Lorenzo, the style is much more alternative.

Treasure Hunt

Rome has a huge array of specialist shops, fashion boutiques and artisanal workshops, with a particularly impressive portfolio of food, clothing and accessory boutiques. Many of these businesses are family owned, having been passed down through the generations. Others have grown from their modest origins into global brands.

What to Buy

Rome is a top place to shop for designer clothes, shoes and leather goods. Foodie treats are another obvious choice and you'll find no end of delis, bakeries, *pasticcerie* (pastry shops) and chocolate shops. Homeware is another Italian speciality, and many shops focus on covetable kitchenware and sleek interior design.

Shopping Areas

For designer clothes head to Via dei Condotti (pictured) and the streets around Piazza di Spagna. You'll find vintage shops and fashion boutiques on Via del Governo Vecchio and around Campo de' Fiori in the *centro storico,* and in the Monti district. Testaccio is a good bet for foodie purchases, with one of Rome's best delis and a daily market.

Artisans

Rome has a surprising number of artists and artisans who create their goods on the spot in hidden workshops. There are a number of good options in Tridente (try Via Margutta, Via dell'Oca and Via della Penna) and in Monti (try Via del Boschetto and Via Panisperna).

Best Fashion

Atelier Livia Risi Comfortable, stylish and adaptable pieces off the rack or made to measure. (p171)

Bomba Family-operated atelier and boutique selling gorgeous clothing. (p109)

Chiara Baschieri Elegant, beautifully tailored womenswear by a young Roman designer. (p110)

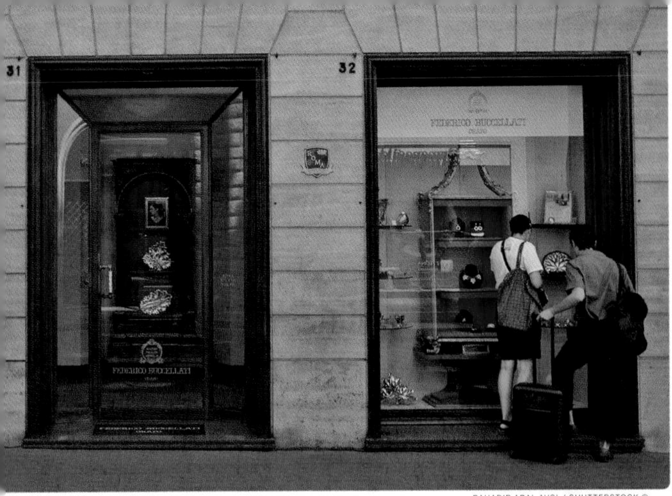

Gente An emporium-style, multi-label boutique. (p109)

Tina Sondergaard Retro-inspired dresses in bijou Monti boutique. (p129)

Best Artisanal

Artisanal Cornucopia Concept store showcasing artisan pieces by Italian designers. (p110)

Flumen Profumi Artisan fragrances with a 'made in Rome' couture label. (p110)

Ibiz – Artigianato in Cuoio Father-and-daughter workshop producing leather wallets, bags and sandals. (p71)

Il Sellaio Beautifully crafted leather bags, belts and accessories. (p91)

Perlei Artisan-made jewellery with a modernist aesthetic. (p129)

Best Gourmet Food

Antica Caciara Trasteverina Wonderful, century-old deli in Trastevere. (p170)

Confetteria Moriondo & Gariglio A 19th-century shop specialising in handmade chocolates. (p71)

Salumeria Roscioli Byword for foodie excellence, with mouth-watering delicacies. (p70)

Volpetti Bulging with delicious delicacies, with notably helpful staff. (p151)

Top Tips

- Many city-centre shops close on Monday morning.
- Winter sales run from early January to mid-February, and summer sales from July to early September.

History

For thousands of years Rome was at the centre of world events. First, as caput mundi *(capital of the world), the glittering hub of the vast Roman Empire, and then as the seat of papal power. It was a city that counted – and this is writ large on its historic streets, where every* palazzo*, church and ancient ruin has a tale to tell.*

Ancient Glories

Many of Rome's most thrilling monuments hark back to its golden age as *caput mundi* (capital of the world), the hub of the Roman Empire. The Colosseum, Pantheon, Roman Forum – these epic ruins all tell of past glories in a way that no textbook ever could.

Church Rule

For much of its history, the Church called the shots in Rome and many of the city's top sights are religious in origin. Early basilicas stand testament to the tenacity of the Church's founding fathers, while the masterpieces that litter the city's churches testify to the wealth and ambition of the Renaissance and baroque-era popes.

Layers of History

One of Rome's characteristic features is the way history literally rises from the ground. Over the centuries the city has undergone various transformations and with each one a new layer was added to the city's urban fabric. As a result, medieval churches stand over pagan temples and baroque piazzas sit atop Roman arenas.

Best Roman Relics

Colosseum Rome's iconic amphitheatre encapsulates all the drama of ancient Rome. (p36)

Pantheon This awe-inspiring temple has served as an architectural blueprint for millennia. (p54)

Terme di Caracalla The hulking remains of this baths complex are among Rome's most impressive. (p147)

Roman Forum The inspiring ruins of ancient Rome's showpiece city centre. (p40)

DI GREGORIO GIULIO / SHUTTERSTOCK ©

Best Underground

Basilica di San Clemente A medieval basilica set atop a pagan temple and 1st-century house. (p137)

Catacombs Via Appia Antica is riddled with catacombs where the early Christians buried their dead. (p154)

Le Domus Romane di Palazzo Valentini Excavated ruins extend beneath a stately 16th-century mansion. (p103)

Best Churches

St Peter's Basilica The Vatican's showpiece church stands over St Peter's tomb. (p80)

Basilica di San Giovanni in Laterano The main papal basilica until the 14th century. (p134)

Basilica di San Paolo Fuori le Mura Monumental basilica on the site where St Paul was buried. (pictured; p153)

Chiesa del Gesù Important Jesuit church, home to Ignatius Loyola for 12 years. (p65)

Best Legendary Sites

Palatino Where the wolf saved Romulus and Remus, and Rome was founded in 753 BC. (p47)

Bocca della Verità Tell a lie and the 'Mouth of Truth' will bite your hand off. (p50)

Worth a Trip

Rome's answer to Pompeii, the **Area Archeologica di Ostia Antica** www.ostia antica.beniculturali.it/; Viale dei Romagnoli 717; adult/reduced €10/5; ⌚8.30am-7.15pm Tue-Sun summer, last admission 6.15pm, shorter hours winter) offers a well-preserved insight into ancient Rome's once-thriving port. To get there, take the train from Stazione Porta San Paolo (by Piramide metro station).

Art & Museums

Home to some of the world's greatest art, Rome is a visual feast. Its churches contain priceless masterpieces and its museums are laden with instantly recognisable works. From classical statues and Renaissance frescoes to baroque sculptures and futuristic paintings, the art on show spans almost 3000 years of artistic endeavour.

Classical Art

Not surprisingly, Rome's collection of ancient art – largely comprising sculpture, commemorative reliefs, and mosaics – is unparalleled. The Vatican Museums and Capitoline Museums showcase much of the city's finest classical sculpture, but you'll also find superlative pieces at Palazzo Altemps and Palazzo Massimo alle Terme.

Renaissance

The Renaissance unleashed an artistic maelstrom in early 16th-century Rome as powerful Church patrons commissioned artists such as Michelangelo and Raphael to decorate the city's basilicas and palaces. Many celebrated frescoes date to this period, including Michelangelo's Sistine Chapel paintings (in the Vatican Museums).

The Baroque

The baroque burst onto Rome's art scene in the early 17th century and was enthusiastically adopted by the Church as a propaganda tool in its battle against Reformation heresy. Works by the period's two leading artists – Gian Lorenzo Bernini and controversial painter Caravaggio – adorn churches and museums across the city.

Best Museums

Vatican Museums The Sistine Chapel and Raphael Rooms headline at this spectacular museum complex. (p74)

Museo e Galleria Borghese Houses Rome's best baroque sculpture and some superlative Old Masters. (p112)

Capitoline Museums Ancient sculpture is the main draw at the world's oldest public museums. (p47)

STEVE HEAP / SHUTTERSTOCK ©

Museo Nazionale Romano: Palazzo Massimo alle Terme Overlooked gem housing fabulous Roman sculpture and mosaics. (p118)

Gallerie Nazionali: Palazzo Barberini Baroque palace laden with paintings by Caravaggio, Raphael, Hans Holbein, Pietro da Cortona et al. (p100)

Galleria Doria Pamphilj Lavish gallery full of major works by big-name Italian and Flemish artists. (p64)

Best Church Art

Sistine Chapel Michelangelo's frescoes are among the world's most famous works of art. (p74)

St Peter's Basilica Marvel at Michelangelo's *Pietà* and many other celebrated masterpieces. (p80)

Chiesa di San Luigi dei Francesi Baroque church home to a trio of moody Caravaggio paintings. (p63)

Basilica di Santa Maria del Popolo Works by Caravaggio, Raphael and Bernini adorn this Renaissance church. (p102)

Basilica di Santa Maria in Trastevere Ancient basilica ablaze with golden apse mosaics. (pictured; p160)

Best Under-the-Radar Museums

Museo Nazionale Etrusco di Villa Giulia Showcases Italy's finest collection of Etruscan treasures. (p114)

Mercati di Traiano Museo dei Fori Imperiali Set in Trajan's towering 2nd-century forum complex. (p50)

Top Tips

- Most museums are closed on Monday.
- State museums are free for under-18s and discounted for EU nationals aged 18 to 25. Take ID as proof of age.

Architecture

BELENOS / SHUTTERSTOCK ©

With ancient ruins, Renaissance basilicas, baroque churches and fascist palazzi (mansions), Rome's architectural legacy is unparalleled. Michelangelo, Bramante, Borromini and Bernini have all stamped their genius on its remarkable cityscape, while in recent years several top architects have completed projects in the city.

Best Ancient Sites

Colosseum Rome's iconic arena bears all the hallmarks of ancient Roman architecture: arches, building materials, unprecedented scale. (p36)

Pantheon The dome, one of the Romans' greatest innovations, finds perfect form atop this revolutionary structure. (p54)

Terme di Caracalla These looming ruins hint at the sophistication of ancient building techniques. (p147)

Mercati di Traiano Museo dei Fori Imperiali A towering model of 2nd-century civic engineering. (p50)

Best Early Basilicas

Basilica di San Giovanni in Laterano Its design set the style for basilicas to follow. (p134)

Basilica di Santa Maria Maggiore The only Roman patriarchal basilica to retain its original layout. (p123)

Best Renaissance Styling

St Peter's Basilica An amalgamation of designs, styles and plans capped by Michelangelo's extraordinary dome. (p80)

Palazzo Farnese Home to the French Embassy, this is a fine example of a classical Renaissance palace. (p65)

Piazza del Campidoglio Michelangelo's hilltop piazza is a show-stopping example of Renaissance town planning. (p47)

Best Baroque Gems

St Peter's Square Bernini designed the Vatican's focal square to funnel believers into St Peter's Basilica. (p89)

Piazza Navona With a Borromini church as well as a Bernini fountain, this celebrated square is a model of baroque beauty. (pictured; p62)

Culture

The Romans have long been passionate about culture. Ever since crowds flocked to the Colosseum for gladiatorial games, the locals have enjoyed a good show, and cultural events draw knowledgeable and enthusiastic audiences. Rome has everything from opera to hip-hop, Shakespearean drama to avant-garde installations.

GLORIA IMBROGNO / SHUTTERSTOCK ©

Best Classical Venues

Auditorium Parco della Musica Great acoustics, top international musicians and multiple concert halls. (pictured; p114)

Teatro dell'Opera di Roma Red velvet and gilt interior for Rome's opera and dance companies. (p129)

Terme di Caracalla Wonderful outdoor setting for summer opera and ballet. (p151)

Best Live Music

Nuovo Cinema Palazzo Exciting creative happenings in a former cinema. (p131)

Blackmarket Hall Two bars filled with vintage sofas, great for eclectic, mainly acoustic, live music. (p127)

ConteStaccio Free live music on the Testaccio clubbing strip. (p151)

Fonclea Prati pub with live gigs featuring everything from rock to doo-wop. (p91)

Best Jazz

Alexanderplatz Rome's foremost jazz club stages international and local musicians. (p91)

Charity Café Spindly tables and chairs, in an intimate space, hosting regular live gigs. (p129)

Big Mama An atmospheric Trastevere venue for jazz, blues, funk, soul and R&B. (p163)

Gregory's Jazz Club This smooth venue near the Spanish Steps is popular with local musicians. (p108)

Top Tips

- Check listings on www.060608.it, www.romeing.it or www.inromenow.com.

- For tickets, try **Vivaticket** (☎892 234; www.vivaticket.it) or **Orbis Servizi** (☎06 482 74 03; www.boxofficelazio.it; Piazza dell'Esquilino 37; ⏰9.30am-1pm & 4-7.30pm Mon-Sat; Ⓜ Termini).

Tours

Taking a guided tour is an excellent way of seeing a lot in a short time or investigating a sight in depth. In high season, book tours in advance.

MAICA / GETTY IMAGES ©

Best Walking Tours

A Friend in Rome (340 5019201; www.afriendinrome.it) Silvia Prosperi and her team offer a range of private tours covering the Vatican and main historic centre, plus areas outside the capital.

The Tour Guy (342 8761859; https://theromanguy.com) Packages, led by English-speaking experts, include skip-the-line visits to the city's top sights and foodie tours of Trastevere.

Best Bike or Scooter Tours

Red Bicycle (327 5387148; www.theredbicycle.org; Via Ostilia 4b; Via Labicana) A cycle outfit offering a range of cycling tours in and around the city.

Bici & Baci (06 482 84 43; www.bicibaci.com; Via del Viminale 5; bike tours from €30, Vespa tours from €145; 8am-7pm; M Repubblica) Runs daily bike tours taking in the main historical sites. Also tours on vintage Vespas, classic Fiat 500 cars, three-wheeled Ape Calessinos.

Best Bus Tours

Open Bus Vatican & Rome (www.operaromanapellegrinaggi.org/it/roma-cristiana/open-bus-vatican-rome; tour €12, 24-/48-hr ticket €25/28) A hop-on, hop-off bus with stops near main sights, including St Peter's Basilica, Piazza Navona and the Colosseum.

Top Tip

An advantage of taking a tour of a big sight is that you'll avoid having to queue for a ticket and you'll skip the line to get in. You might also gain access to parts not usually open to the public.

Under the Radar Rome

From the Colosseum to the Sistine Chapel, Rome's historic sites are among the most visited in Italy. That means crowds and the risk of over-tourism, particularly in peak periods. To avoid the queues and discover another side of Rome, set your sights on the city's lesser-known gems and neighbourhoods.

WILL SALTER / LONELY PLANET ©

Best Alternative Neighbourhoods

Testaccio Once-proletarian Testaccio is a foodie hotspot with popular trattorias and a busy neighbourhood market. (p134)

Ostiense Against a backdrop of street art and industrial landmarks, Ostiense harbours hot clubs and hip bars as well as several cultural gems. (p152)

Garbatella Full of colour, Garbatella is known for its eclectic architecture, lush courtyards and eye-catching street murals. (p153)

EUR In Rome's southern reaches, EUR is a world apart with its muscular modern architecture (pictured).

San Lorenzo Hang out with the students in left-field San Lorenzo, packed with craft-beer bars, grungy music venues and basement dives. (p130)

Best Off the Beaten Track

Cimitero Acattolico per gli Stranieri Pay homage to romantic poets and socialist thinkers at this peaceful Testaccio oasis. (p148)

Centrale Montemartini Ancient sculpture sidles up to heavy industrial machinery at this de-commissioned power station in Ostiense. (p153)

Chiesa di Santo Stefano Rotondo A secluded church on the Celio hosting a chilling cycle of 16th-century frescoes. (p137)

Basilica di Santa Prassede Be bowled over by dazzling Byzantine mosaics at this easy-to-miss Esquilino church. (p123)

For Kids

NIKADECAROLIS / SHUTTERSTOCK ©

Despite a reputation as a highbrow cultural destination, Rome has a lot to offer kids. Child-specific sights might be thin on the ground, but if you know where to go, there's plenty to keep the little 'uns occupied and parents happy.

Best Museums & Sites for Kids

Explora – Museo dei Bambini di Roma (☎06 361 37 76; www.mdbr.it; Via Flaminia 80-86; €8, children 1-3yr €5, under 1yr free; ⏰entrance 10am, noon, 3pm & 5pm Tue-Sun, no 10am entrance in Aug; MFlaminio) Rome's only dedicated kids' museum, Explora is aimed at the under-12s. It's divided into thematic sections, and with everything from a play pool and fire engine to a train driver's cabin, it's a hands-on, feet-on, full-on experience that your nippers will love. Outside there's also a free play park open to all. Booking is recommended for the timed entrance and required on weekends.

Bioparco (☎06 360 82 11; www.bioparco.it; Viale del Giardino Zoologico 1; adult/reduced €16/13; ⏰9.30am-6pm summer, to 5pm winter; 🚋Bioparco) Rome's zoo hosts a predictable collection of animals, with 200 species from five continents housed on its 18-hectare site in Villa Borghese.

Museo delle Cere (Wax Museum; ☎06 679 64 82; www.museodellecereroma.com; Piazza dei Santissimi Apostoli 68a; adult/reduced €10/8; ⏰9am-9pm summer, to 8pm winter; 👪) Rome's waxwork museum is said to have the world's third-largest collection, which comprises more than 250 figures, ranging from Dante to Snow White, plus plentiful popes, poets, politicians, musicians and murderers. Don't miss the laboratory where the waxworks are created.

Top Tips

- Under-18s get in free at state-run museums; city-run museums are free for under-sixes and discounted for six- to 25-year-olds.
- Under-10s travel free on public transport.

LGBTIQ+ Rome

KRAFT74 / SHUTTERSTOCK ©

Rome has a thriving, if low-key, gay scene. There are relatively few queer-only venues, but the Colosseum end of Via di San Giovanni in Laterano is a favourite hang-out and many clubs host regular gay and lesbian nights. Outside town, there are a couple of popular gay beaches at Ostia: Settimo Cielo and the Oasi Naturista Capocotta.

Best Events

Gay Village (350 0723346; www.gayvillage.it; Lungotevere Testacci; €3-20; 7.30pm-3.30am Thu-Sat Jun-early Sep; M Piramide) Rome's big annual LGBTIQ+ festival attracts crowds of partygoers and an exuberant cast of DJs, musicians and entertainers. It serves up an eclectic mix of dance music, film screenings, cultural debates and theatrical performances.

Best Venues

Coming Out (06 700 98 71; www.comingout.it; Via di San Giovanni in Laterano 8; 7am-5.30am; Via Labicana) On warm evenings, with lively crowds on the street and the Colosseum as a backdrop, there are few finer places to sip a drink than this friendly gay bar. It's open all day, but is at its best in the evening when the atmosphere hots up, the cocktails kick in and the karaoke and speed dating get under way.

L'Alibi (320 3541185; Via di Monte Testaccio 44; 11pm-4am Thu, 11.30pm-5am Fri & Sat; Via Galvani) Gay-friendly L'Alibi is one of Rome's best-known clubs, hosting regular parties and serving up a mash of house, hip-hop, Latino, pop and dance music to a young, mixed crowd. It can get pretty steamy inside, particularly on packed weekend nights, but you can grab a mouthful of air on the spacious summer terrace.

Top Tip

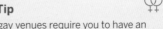

Most gay venues require you to have an Arcigay membership card. These cost €10 from the **Arcigay** (06 6450 1102; www.arcigayroma.it; Via Nicola Zabaglia 14; 4-8pm Mon-Sat) headquarters in Testaccio or any venue that requires one.

Four Perfect Days

Day 1

VIACHESLAV LOPATIN / SHUTTERSTOCK ©

Start the day at the **Colosseum** (p36), Rome's huge gladiatorial arena. Then head to the **Palatino** (p47) to poke around ancient ruins, before descending into the **Roman Forum** (p40).

After lunch at **Terre e Domus** (p51), stop by **Piazza del Campidoglio** (p47) and the **Capitoline Museums** (pictured; p47), where you'll find some sensational ancient sculpture. Done there, enjoy views from the **Vittoriano** (p48) before pressing on to the **Pantheon** (p54) and **Piazza Navona** (p62).

Spend the evening in the *centro storico* (historic centre): dine at **La Ciambella** (p67), then chat over coffee at **Caffè Sant'Eustachio** (p68).

Day 2

MARC RASMUS / GETTY IMAGES ©

First up on day two are the **Vatican Museums** (p74). Once you've blown your mind on the Sistine Chapel and the myriad other masterpieces, complete your Vatican tour at **St Peter's Basilica** (p80).

After lunching on sliced pizza at **Bonci Pizzarium** (p89), jump on the metro to **Piazza di Spagna** (p96). Plan your moves while sitting on the **Spanish Steps** (p96), then push on to the **Trevi Fountain** (p94). Next, head up the hill for sunset views on **Piazza del Quirinale** (p107) by the presidential Palazzo del Quirinale.

Finish the day off in the area around **Campo de' Fiori** (pictured; p69). Try **Open Baladin** (p68) for craft beers or **Barnum Cafe** (p69) for chilled cocktails.

Day 3

BWZENITH / GETTY IMAGES ©

Day three starts with a trip to the **Museo e Galleria Borghese** (p112) to marvel at amazing baroque sculpture and Renaissance masterpieces. Afterwards, take a stroll through Rome's central park, **Villa Borghese** (pictured; p114).

In the afternoon, press on to **Piazza del Popolo** (p101) to catch a couple of Caravaggios at the **Basilica di Santa Maria del Popolo** (p102). Next, dedicate some time to browsing the flagship stores and designer boutiques in the upscale streets off **Via del Corso**.

Over the river, the picture-perfect **Trastevere** neighbourhood bursts with life in the evening. Hotspots include **Terra Satis** (p169), a laid-back wine bar, and mellow **Niji Roma** (p163).

Day 4

PEN_85 / SHUTTERSTOCK ©

On day four, venture out to **Via Appia Antica** (p154) where you can go underground in the **catacombs** (p155) and poke around ancient ruins at the **Villa di Massenzio** (p156).

Done there, head back to Stazione Termini and the nearby **Museo Nazionale Romano: Palazzo Massimo alle Terme** (p118) for some classical sculpture and stunning mosaics. Then, drop by the **Basilica di Santa Maria Maggiore** (pictured; p123) and **Basilica di San Pietro in Vincoli** (p124), home to Michelangelo's Moses sculpture. Finish up with some shopping in the fashionable **Monti** district.

Stay put in Monti in the evening. After dinner at **La Barrique** (p126), pick a bar or cafe to see out the day.

Need to Know

For detailed information, see Survival Guide p173

Currency
euro (€)

Language
Italian

Visas
Generally not required for stays of up to 90 days.

Money
ATMs are widespread. Major credit cards are widely accepted but smaller businesses might not take them.

Mobile Phones
Local SIM cards can be used in European, Australian and unlocked US phones. Other phones must be set to roaming.

Time
Western European Time (GMT/UTC plus one hour)

Tipping
Not necessary, but round the bill up in pizzerias/trattorias or leave a euro or two; five to 10% is fine in smarter restaurants.

Daily Budget

Budget: Less than €110

Dorm bed: €15–45

Double room in a budget hotel: €60–130

Pizza plus beer: €15

Midrange: €110–250

Double room in a hotel: €100–200

Local restaurant meal: €25–45

Admission to Vatican Museums: €17

Roma Pass, a 72-hour card covering museum entry and public transport: €38.50

Top end: More than €250

Double room in a four- or five-star hotel: €200 plus

Top restaurant dinner: €45–160

Opera ticket: €17–150

City-centre taxi ride: €10–15

Auditorium concert tickets: €20–90

Advance Planning

Two months before Book high-season accommodation.

One month before Check for concerts at www.auditorium.com. Book tickets for Colosseum tours and visits to the Museo e Galleria Borghese and Palazzo Farnese.

One to two weeks before Reserve tickets for the pope's weekly audience at St Peter's.

Few days before Reserve tables at top restaurants. Book tickets for the Vatican Museums and Colosseum (advisable to avoid queues).

Arriving in Rome

Most people arrive by plane at one of Rome's two airports: Leonardo da Vinci, better known as Fiumicino, or Ciampino, hub for Ryanair. Trains serve Rome's main station, Stazione Termini, from a number of European destinations, including Paris (about 15 hours), as well as cities across Italy.

From Leonardo da Vinci (Fiumicino) Airport

30km west of the city centre:

Leonardo Express trains to Stazione Termini 6.08am to 11.23pm, €14

Slower FL1 trains to Trastevere, Ostiense and Tiburtina stations 5.57am to 10.42pm, €8

Buses to Stazione Termini 6.05am to 12.40am, €6-6.90

Airport-to-hotel shuttles from €22 per person

Taxis €48 (fixed fare to within the Aurelian walls)

From Ciampino Airport

15km southeast of the city centre:

Buses to Stazione Termini 4am to 12.15am, €6

Airport-to-hotel shuttles €25 per person

Taxis €30 (fixed fare to within the Aurelian walls)

From Stazione Termini

Near the city centre:

Airport buses and **trains**, and international trains, arrive at Stazione Termini. From there, continue by bus, metro or taxi.

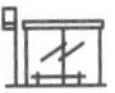

Getting Around

Public transport includes buses, trams, metro and suburban trains. The main hub is Stazione Termini. Tickets, which come in various forms, are valid for all forms of transport. Children under 10 travel free.

Metro

The metro is quicker than surface transport, but the network is limited. Two main lines serve the centre, A (orange) and B (blue), crossing at Stazione Termini. Trains run between 5.30am and 11.30pm (to 1.30am Friday and Saturday).

Bus

Most routes pass through Stazione Termini. Buses run from approximately 5.30am until midnight, with limited services throughout the night.

Walk

Walking is the best way of getting around the *centro storico* (historic centre).

Rome Neighbourhoods

Vatican City, Borgo & Prati (p73)
Feast on extravagant art in the monumental Vatican and excellent food in neighbouring Prati.

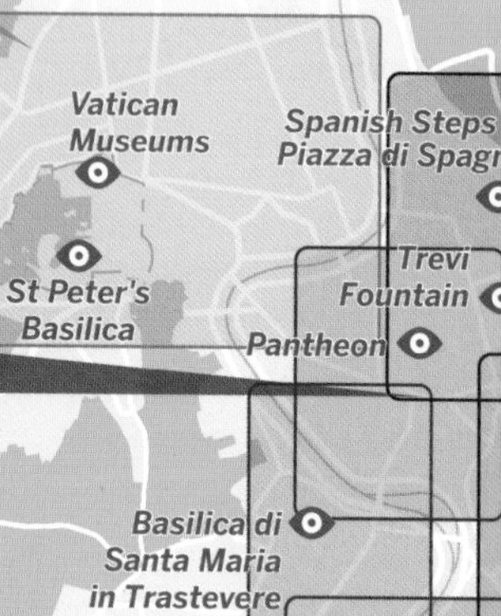

Centro Storico (p53)
Rome's historic centre is the capital's thumping heart – a heady warren of famous squares and tangled lanes, galleries, restaurants and bars.

Trastevere & Gianicolo (p159)
Trastevere's medieval streets heave with kicking bars and eateries. The Gianicolo offers to-die-for panoramas.

Aventino & Testaccio (p143)
Ideal for a romantic getaway, hilltop Aventino rises above Testaccio, famous for its nose-to-tail cooking and thumping nightlife.

Museo e Galleria Borghese

Museo Nazionale Romano: Palazzo Massimo alle Terme

Roman Forum

Colosseum

Basilica di San Giovanni in Laterano

Via Appia Antica

Tridente, Trevi & the Quirinale (p93)
Debonair, touristy area boasting a presidential palace, Rome's most famous fountain, designer boutiques and swish bars.

Monti & Esquilino (p117)
Boutiques and wine bars abound in Monti, while Esquilino offers multiculturalism and several must-see museums and churches.

Ancient Rome (p35)
Rome's ancient core is a beautiful area of evocative ruins, improbable legends, soaring pine trees and panoramic views.

San Giovanni & Celio (p133)
Explore medieval churches and escape the tourist crowds in residential San Giovanni and on the leafy Celio hill.

Explore Rome

Worth a Trip

Rome's Walking Tours

Piazza Navona (p62) NICOLA FORENZA / GETTY IMAGES ©

Explore Ancient Rome

In a city of extraordinary beauty, Rome's ancient heart stands out. It's here you'll find the great icons of the city's past: the Colosseum; the Palatino; the forums; and the Campidoglio (Capitoline Hill), the historic home of the Capitoline Museums. Touristy by day, it's quiet at night with few after-hours attractions.

The Short List

- ***Colosseum (p36)*** *Getting your first glimpse of Rome's iconic amphitheatre.*
- ***Palatino (p47)*** *Exploring the haunting ruins of the Palatine Hill, ancient Rome's birthplace and most exclusive neighbourhood.*
- ***Capitoline Museums (p47)*** *Going face to face with centuries of awe-inspiring art at the world's oldest public museums.*
- ***Roman Forum (p40)*** *Exploring the basilicas, temples and triumphal arches of what was once the nerve centre of the Roman Empire.*
- ***Vittoriano (p48)*** *Surveying the city spread out beneath you from atop this colossal marble extravaganza.*

Getting There & Around

Buses 40, 64, 87, 170, 916 and H to Piazza Venezia. Bus 87 runs along Via dei Fori Imperiali between the Colosseum and Vittoriano.

M Line B for the Colosseum (Colosseo) and Circo Massimo. If taking the metro at Termini, follow signs for Line B 'direzione Laurentina'.

Ancient Rome Map on p46

The Cordonata staircase (p48) SUN_SHINE / SHUTTERSTOCK ©

Top Experience 

Tour the Colosseum

An awesome, spine-tingling sight, the Colosseum is the most thrilling of Rome's ancient monuments. It was here that gladiators met in mortal combat and condemned prisoners fought off wild beasts in front of baying, bloodthirsty crowds. Two thousand years on and it's Italy's top tourist attraction, drawing more than seven million visitors a year.

MAP P46, D4

Colosseo

www.parcocolosseo.it

Piazza del Colosseo

adult/reduced incl Forum & Palatino €12/7.50

8.30am-1hr before sunset

M Colosseo

History

The emperor Vespasian (r AD 69–79) originally commissioned the amphitheatre in AD 72 in the grounds of Nero's vast Domus Aurea complex. He never lived to see it finished, though, and it was completed by his son and successor Titus (r 79–81) in AD 80. To mark its inauguration, Titus held games that lasted 100 days and nights, during which some 5000 animals were slaughtered. Trajan (r 98–117) later topped this, holding a marathon 117-day killing spree involving 9000 gladiators and 10,000 animals.

The 50,000-seat arena was Rome's first, and greatest, permanent amphitheatre. For some five centuries it was used to stage lavish, crowd-pleasing spectacles to mark important anniversaries or military victories. Gladiatorial combat was eventually outlawed in the 5th century but wild animal shows continued until the mid-6th century.

Following the fall of the Roman Empire, the Colosseum was largely abandoned. It was used as a fortress by the powerful Frangipani family in the 12th century and later plundered of its precious building materials. Travertine and marble stripped from the Colosseum were used to decorate a number of Rome's notable buildings, including Palazzo Venezia, Palazzo Barberini and Palazzo Cancelleria.

More recently, pollution and vibrations caused by traffic and the metro have taken a toll. To help counter this, the amphitheatre was given a major clean-up between 2014 and 2016 – the first in its 2000-year history – as part of an ongoing €25-million restoration project sponsored by the luxury shoemaker Tod's.

The Exterior

The outer walls have three levels of arches, framed by decorative columns topped by capitals of the Ionic (at the bottom), Doric and Corinthian (at the top) orders. They were

★ Top Tips

- Visit early morning or late afternoon to avoid the crowds.
- If queues are long, get your ticket at the Palatino, about 250m away at Via di San Gregorio 30.
- Other queue-jumping tips: book tickets online at www.coopculture.it (plus €2 booking fee); get the Roma Pass or SUPER ticket; join a tour (see www.coopculture.it for options).
- Basic full-price admission tickets can be pre-printed; others (reduced/free/tours) must be picked up on site.

✕ Take a Break

Avoid the rip-off restaurants in the immediate vicinity. Instead push on to the area east of the Colosseum for a light casual meal at Cafè Cafè (p139).

originally covered in travertine, and marble statues filled the niches on the 2nd and 3rd storeys. The upper level, punctuated with windows and slender Corinthian pilasters, had supports for 240 masts that held the awning over the arena, shielding the spectators from sun and rain. The 80 entrance arches, known as *vomitoria,* allowed the spectators to enter and be seated in a matter of minutes.

The Seating

The *cavea,* or spectator seating, was divided into three tiers: magistrates and senior officials sat in the lowest tier, wealthy citizens in the middle and the plebs in the highest tier. Women (except for Vestal Virgins) were relegated to the cheapest sections at the top. Tickets were numbered and spectators were assigned a precise seat in a specific sector – in 2015, restorers uncovered traces of red numerals on the arches, indicating how the sectors were numbered.

The podium, a broad terrace in front of the tiers of seats, was reserved for the emperor, senators and VIPs.

After a long period of closure, the top three rings, known collectively as the Belvedere, are now open and can be visited on guided tours.

The Arena

The stadium originally had a wooden floor covered in sand – *harena* in Latin, hence the word 'arena' – to prevent combatants from slipping and to soak up spilt blood.

Interior

CHANDRADHAS / GETTY IMAGES ©

Colosseum Curiosities

The Name

The arena was originally known as the Flavian Amphitheatre (Anfiteatro di Flavio) after Vespasian's family name. And while it was Rome's most famous arena, it wasn't the biggest – the Circo Massimo could hold up to 250,000 people. The name Colosseum, when introduced in the Middle Ages, wasn't a reference to its size but to the Colosso di Nerone, a giant statue of Nero that stood nearby.

Gladiatorial Games

Games staged here usually involved gladiators fighting wild animals or each other. But contrary to Hollywood folklore, bouts rarely ended in death as the games' sponsor was required to pay compensation to a gladiator's owner if the gladiator died in action.

Trapdoors led down to the hypogeum, a subterranean complex of corridors, cages and lifts beneath the arena floor.

Hypogeum

The hypogeum served as the stadium's backstage area. It was here that stage sets were prepared and combatants, both human and animal, would gather before showtime. Gladiators entered from the nearby Ludus Magnus (gladiator school) via an underground corridor, whilst a second tunnel, the Passaggio di Commodo (Passage of Commodus), allowed the emperor to arrive without having to pass through the crowds.

To hoist people, animals and scenery up to the arena, the hypogeum was equipped with a sophisticated network of 80 winch-operated lifts, all controlled by a single pulley system.

Visits to the hypogeum are by guided tour only. These can be booked online at www.coopculture.it and cost €9 (or €15 including the Belvedere) on top of the normal Colosseum ticket.

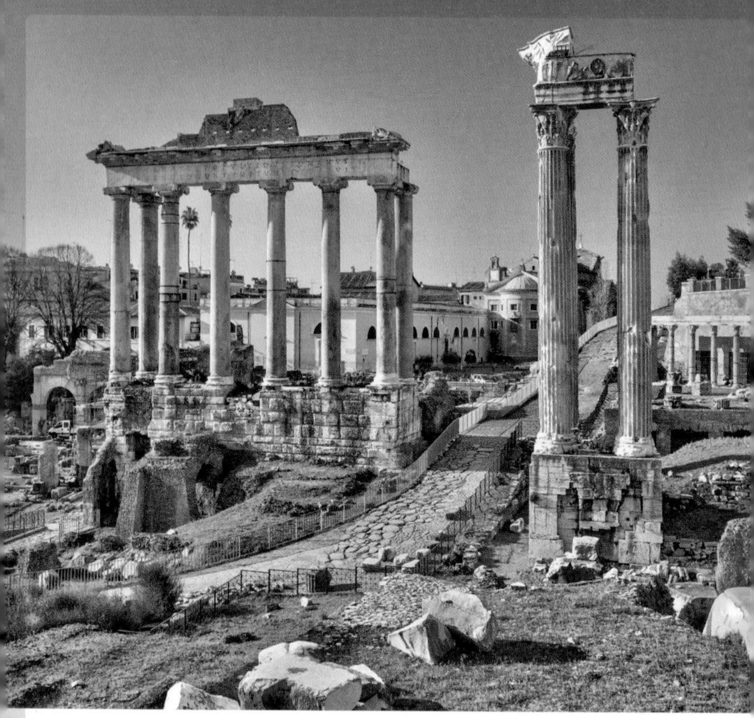

Top Experience

Wander through the Roman Forum

This was ancient Rome's showpiece centre, a grandiose district of temples, basilicas and vibrant public spaces. Nowadays, it's a collection of impressive, if sketchily labelled, ruins that can leave you confused. But if you can get your imagination going, there's something wonderfully compelling about walking in the footsteps of Julius Caesar and other legendary figures of Roman history.

MAP P46, B3

Foro Romano

www.parcocolosseo.it

Largo della Salara Vecchia, Piazza di Santa Maria Nova

adult/reduced incl Colosseum & Palatino €12/7.50

8.30am-1hr before sunset

Via dei Fori Imperiali

Via Sacra & Tempio di Giulio Cesare

As you enter from Largo della Salara Vecchia, a path leads down to **Via Sacra**, the Forum's main thoroughfare, and the **Tempio di Giulio Cesare** (aka Tempio del Divo Giulio). Built by Augustus in 29 BC, this marks the spot where Caesar was cremated after his assassination in 44 BC.

Curia

Heading right up Via Sacra brings you to the **Curia**, the original seat of the Roman Senate. This barn-like construction was rebuilt on various occasions and what you see today is a 1937 reconstruction of how it looked in the reign of Diocletian (r 284–305).

Arco di Settimio Severo & Rostri

At the end of Via Sacra, the 23m-high **Arco di Settimio Severo** (Arch of Septimius Severus) is dedicated to the eponymous emperor and his two sons, Caracalla and Geta. Built in AD 203, it commemorates Roman victories over the Parthians.

Close by are the remains of the **Rostri** (Rostra), an elaborate podium where local politicos would harangue the market crowds.

Facing the Rostri, the **Colonna di Foca** (Column of Phocus) rises above what was once the Forum's main square, **Piazza del Foro**.

Tempio di Saturno

Eight granite columns are all that survive of the **Tempio di Saturno** (Temple of Saturn), one of the Forum's landmark sights. Inaugurated in 497 BC and subsequently rebuilt in the 1st century BC, it was an important temple that doubled as the state treasury.

★ Top Tips

- Get grandstand views of the Forum from the Palatino and Campidoglio.
- Visit first thing in the morning or late afternoon; crowds are worst between 11am and 2pm.
- In summer it gets very hot and there's little shade, so take a hat and plenty of water. Comfortable shoes are a must.
- If you're caught short, there are toilets by the Chiesa di Santa Maria Antiqua.
- To enter the Chiesa di Santa Maria Antiqua, Rampa di Domiziano and Tempio di Romolo you'll need the SUPER ticket (p47).

✕ Take a Break

For a coffee break, head to the Terrazza Caffarelli (p51), the Capitoline Museums' panoramic rooftop cafe.

Alternatively, Terre e Domus (p51) serves excellent regional cuisine and fine local wines.

Vestal Virgins

Despite privilege and public acclaim, life as a Vestal Virgin was no bed of roses. Every year, six physically perfect patrician girls aged between six and 10 were chosen by lottery to serve in the Tempio di Vesta for a period of 30 years. If a Vestal were to lose her virginity, she risked being buried alive and her partner in crime being flogged to death.

Tempio di Castore e Polluce

In the centre of the Forum, three columns remain from the 5th-century BC **Tempio di Castore e Polluce** (Temple of Castor and Pollux), dedicated to the heavenly twins Castor and Pollux.

Chiesa di Santa Maria Antiqua

The 6th-century **Chiesa di Santa Maria Antiqua** (SUPER ticket adult/reduced €18/13.50; ⏲9am-6.30pm Tue, Thu & Sat, from 2pm Sun summer, 9am-3.30pm Tue, Thu & Sat, from 2pm Sun winter) is the oldest and most important Christian site on the forum. It's a treasure trove of early Christian art containing exquisite 6th- to 9th-century frescoes and one of the oldest icons in existence.

Casa delle Vestali

The **Casa delle Vestali** (House of the Vestal Virgins) was the home of the virgins who tended the flame in the adjoining **Tempio di Vesta**. At its centre is a rectangular grassy space lined with a string of statues, now mostly headless, depicting the Vestals.

Basilica di Massenzio

The **Basilica di Massenzio** (Basilica di Costantino) is the largest building on the Forum. Started by Maxentius and finished by Constantine in 315, it originally measured 100m by 65m, roughly three times what it now covers.

Arco di Tito

Said to be the inspiration for Paris' Arc de Triomphe, the **Arco di Tito** (Arch of Titus) was built by Domitian in AD 81 to celebrate his brother Titus' military victories in Judea and the AD 70 sack of Jerusalem.

Via Cavour
Via del Colosseo
Via Frangipane
Via del Colosseo
Via del Tempio della Pace
Via dei Fori Imperiali
Largo C Ricci
Via dei Fori Imperiali
Largo della Salara Vecchia
Entrance
Via della Salara Vecchia
Basilica di Massenzio
Via Sacra
Tempio di Giulio Cesare
Via Sacra
Tempio di Castore e Polluce
Tempio di Vesta
Casa delle Vestali
Chiesa di Santa Maria Antiqua
Orti Farnesiani
Arco di Tito
Entrance
Entrance
Via della Curia
Curia
Via di Tulliano
Colonna di Foca
Piazza del Foro
Vicus Tuscus
Rostri
Arco di Settimio Severo
Entrance
Via di San Pietro in Carcere
Tempio di Saturno
Via del Foro Romano
Via del Foro Romano
Via dei Foraggi
Via dei Fienili
Via della Consolazione
Piazza del Campidoglio
0
100 m

Walking Tour

Emperors' Footsteps

Follow in the footsteps of Rome's legendary emperors on this walk around the best of the city's ancient treasures. Established in 27 BC, the Roman Empire grew to become the Western world's first dominant superpower and at the peak of its power, in about AD 100, it extended from Britain to north Africa, and from Syria to Spain.

Walk Facts

Start Colosseum, metro Colosseo

End Vittoriano, bus Piazza Venezia

Length 2km; at least three hours

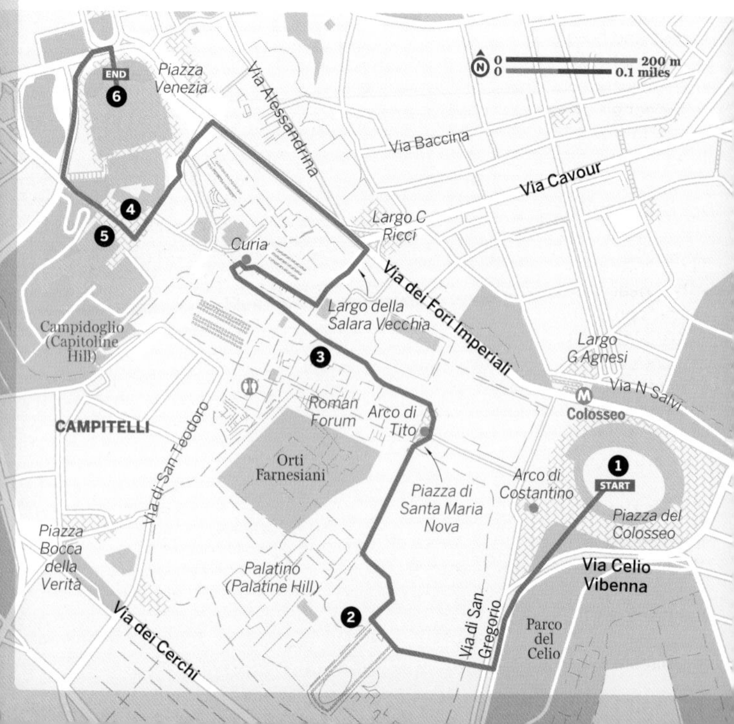

❶ Colosseum

More than any other monument, it's the **Colosseum** (p36) that symbolises the power and glory of ancient Rome. A spectacular feat of engineering, the 50,000-seat stadium was inaugurated by Emperor Titus in AD80 with a bloodthirsty bout of games that lasted 100 days and nights.

❷ Palatino

A short walk from the Colosseum, the **Palatino** (p47) was ancient Rome's most sought-after neighbourhood, site of the emperor's palace and home to the cream of imperial society. The evocative ruins are confusing but their grandeur gives some sense of the luxury in which the ancient VIPs liked to live.

❸ Roman Forum

Coming down from the Palatino you'll enter the **Roman Forum** (p40) near the Arco di Tito, one of Rome's great triumphal arches. In imperial times, the Forum was the empire's nerve centre, a teeming hive of law courts, temples, piazzas and shops. The Vestal Virgins lived here and senators debated matters of state in the Curia.

❹ Piazza del Campidoglio

Exit the Forum at Largo della Salara Vecchia and head up to the Michelangelo-designed **Piazza del Campidoglio** (p47). This striking piazza sits atop the Campidoglio (Capitoline Hill), one of the seven hills on which Rome was founded. In ancient times this was the spiritual heart of the city, home to two of the city's most important temples.

❺ Capitoline Museums

Flanking Piazza del Campidoglio are two stately *palazzi* (mansions) that together house the **Capitoline Museums** (p47). These, the world's oldest public museums, boast an important picture gallery and a superb collection of classical sculpture that includes the iconic *Lupa Capitolina*, a bronze wolf standing over her suckling wards, Romulus and Remus.

❻ Vittoriano

From the Campidoglio, pop next door to the massive mountain of white marble that is the **Vittoriano** (p48). No emperor ever walked here, but it's worth stopping off to take the panoramic lift to the top, from where you can see the whole of Rome laid out beneath you.

✕ Take a Break

Hidden away in the Capitoline Museums but accessible by its own entrance, the **Terrazza Caffarelli** (p51) is a refined spot for a restorative coffee.

For reviews see

Top Experiences	p36
Sights	p47
Eating	p51
Drinking	p51

Sights

Palatino
ARCHAEOLOGICAL SITE

1 MAP P46, C5

Sandwiched between the Roman Forum and the Circo Massimo, the Palatino (Palatine Hill) is one of Rome's most spectacular sights: a beautiful, atmospheric area of towering pine trees, majestic ruins and unforgettable views. This is where Romulus supposedly founded the city in 753 BC and Rome's emperors lived in palatial luxury. Look out for the **stadio** (stadium), the ruins of the **Domus Flavia** (imperial palace), and grandstand views over the Roman Forum from the **Orti Farnesiani**. (Palatine Hill; 06 3996 7700; www.parcocolosseo.it; Via di San Gregorio 30, Piazza di Santa Maria Nova; adult/reduced incl Colosseum & Roman Forum €12/7.50, SUPER ticket €18/13.50; 8.30am-1hr before sunset; some SUPER ticket sites Mon, Wed, Fri & morning Sun only; M Colosseo)

Capitoline Museums
MUSEUM

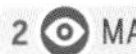
2 MAP P46, A3

Dating from 1471, the Capitoline Museums are the world's oldest public museums. Their collection of classical sculpture is one of Italy's finest, boasting works such as the iconic *Lupa Capitolina* (Capitoline Wolf), a life-size bronze of a she-wolf suckling Romulus and Remus, and the *Galata morente* (Dying Gaul), a moving depiction of a dying warrior.

SUPER Ticket

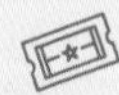

To visit the Palatino and Roman Forum's internal sites you'll need to buy a SUPER ticket and plan carefully. The ticket, valid for two consecutive days, covers the Colosseum, Roman Forum and Palatino. On the Palatino, the Casa di Augusto, Casa di Livia, Aula Isiaca and Loggia Mattei are open on Mondays, Wednesdays, Fridays and Sunday mornings; the Museo Palatino and Criptoportico Neroniano open daily. The Roman Forum sites (Tempio di Romolo, Chiesa di Santa Maria in Antiqua, Rampa di Domiziano) are open on Tuesdays, Thursdays, Saturdays and Sunday afternoons.

There's also a formidable gallery with masterpieces by the likes of Titian, Tintoretto, Rubens and Caravaggio. Ticket prices increase when there's a temporary exhibition on. (Musei Capitolini; 06 06 08; www.museicapitolini.org; Piazza del Campidoglio 1; adult/reduced €11.50/9.50; 9.30am-7.30pm, last admission 6.30pm; Piazza Venezia)

Piazza del Campidoglio
PIAZZA

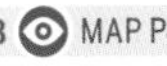
3 MAP P46, A3

This hilltop piazza, designed by Michelangelo in 1538, is one of Rome's most beautiful squares.

There are several approaches but the most dramatic is the graceful **Cordonata** staircase, which leads up from Piazza d'Aracoeli. The piazza is flanked by **Palazzo Nuovo** and **Palazzo dei Conservatori**, together home to the Capitoline Museums, and **Palazzo Senatorio**, Rome's historic city hall. In the centre is a copy of an **equestrian statue** of Marcus Aurelius. (Piazza Venezia)

Vittoriano

MONUMENT

4 MAP P46, A2

Love it or loathe it, as many Romans do, you can't ignore the Vittoriano (aka the Altare della Patria, Altar of the Fatherland), the colossal mountain of white marble that towers over Piazza Venezia. Built at the turn of the 20th century to honour Italy's first king, Vittorio Emanuele II – who's immortalised in its vast equestrian statue – it provides the dramatic setting for the **Tomb of the Unknown Soldier** and, inside, the small **Museo Centrale del Risorgimento** (06 679 35 98; www.risorgimento.it; adult/reduced €5/2.50; 9.30am-6.30pm), documenting Italian unification. (Victor Emanuel Monument; Piazza Venezia; admission free; 9.30am-5.30pm summer, to 4.30pm winter; Piazza Venezia)

Palazzo Venezia

MUSEUM

5 MAP P46, A1

Built between 1455 and 1464, Palazzo Venezia was the first of Rome's great Renaissance palaces.

Vittoriano

A Who's Who of Roman Emperors

Of the 250 or so emperors of the Roman Empire, only a few were truly heroic. Here are 10 of the best, worst and completely insane.

Augustus (27 BC–AD 14) Rome's first emperor. Ushers in a period of peace and security; the arts flourish and many monuments are built.

Caligula (37–41) Emperor number three after Augustus and Tiberius. Remains popular until illness leads to the depraved behaviour for which he becomes infamous. Is murdered by his bodyguards on the Palatino.

Claudius (41–54) Expands the Roman Empire and conquers Britain. Is eventually poisoned, probably at the instigation of Agrippina, his wife and Nero's mother.

Nero (54–68) Initially rules well but later slips into madness – he has his mother murdered, persecutes the Christians and attempts to turn half the city into a palace, the Domus Aurea. He is eventually forced into suicide.

Vespasian (69–79) First of the Flavian dynasty, he imposes peace and cleans up the imperial finances. His greatest legacy is the Colosseum.

Trajan (98–117) Conquers the east and rules over the empire at its zenith. He revamps Rome's city centre, adding a forum, marketplace and column, all of which still stand.

Hadrian (117–38) Puts an end to imperial expansion and constructs walls to mark the empire's borders.

Aurelian (270–75) Does much to control the rebellion that sweeps the empire at the end of the 3rd century. Starts construction of the city walls that still today bear his name.

Diocletian (284–305) Splits the empire into eastern and western halves in 285. Launches a savage persecution of the Christians as he struggles to control the empire's eastern reaches.

Constantine I (306–37) Although based in Byzantium (later renamed Constantinople in his honour), he legalises Christianity.

For centuries it was the embassy of the Venetian Republic – hence its name – but it's most readily associated with Mussolini, who had his office here and famously made speeches from the balcony of the Sala del Mappamondo (Globe Room). Nowadays it's home to the **Museo Nazionale del Palazzo Venezia** and its eclectic collection of Byzantine and early Renaissance paintings, ceramics, bronze figures, weaponry and armour. (06 6999 4388; www.museopalazzovenezia.beniculturali.it; Piazza Venezia 3; adult/reduced €10/5; 8.30am-7.30pm Tue-Sun; Piazza Venezia)

Mercati di Traiano Museo dei Fori Imperiali

MUSEUM

6 MAP P46, B2

This striking museum showcases the **Mercati di Traiano**, the emperor Trajan's towering 2nd-century complex, while also providing a fascinating introduction to the Imperial Forums with multimedia displays, explanatory panels and a smattering of archaeological artefacts. Sculptures, friezes and the occasional bust are set out in rooms opening onto what was once the Great Hall. But more than the exhibits, the real highlight here is the chance to explore the vast structure, which historians believe housed the forums' administrative offices. (06 06 08; www.mercatiditraiano.it; Via IV Novembre 94; adult/reduced incl exhibition €11.50/9.50; 9.30am-7.30pm; Via IV Novembre)

Imperial Forums

ARCHAEOLOGICAL SITE

7 MAP P46, B2

The forums of Trajan, Augustus, Nerva and Caesar are known collectively as the Imperial Forums. They were largely buried when Mussolini bulldozed Via dei Fori Imperiali through the area in 1933, but excavations have since unearthed much of them. The standout sights are the Mercati di Traiano (Trajan's Markets) and the landmark **Colonna Traiana** (Trajan's Column). (Fori Imperiali; 06 06 08; Piazza Santa Maria di Loreto; adult/reduced €4/3, free 1st Sun of month Oct-Mar; by reservation; Via dei Fori Imperiali)

Bocca della Verità

MONUMENT

8 MAP P46, A5

A bearded face carved into a giant marble disc, the Bocca della Verità is one of Rome's most popular curiosities. Legend has it that if you put your hand in the mouth and tell a lie, the Bocca will slam shut and bite it off. The mouth, which was originally part of a fountain, or possibly an ancient manhole cover, now lives in the portico of the **Chiesa di Santa Maria in Cosmedin**, a handsome medieval church. (Mouth of Truth; Piazza Bocca della Verità 18; voluntary donation; 9.30am-5.50pm summer, to 4.50pm winter; Piazza Bocca della Verità)

Eating

Terre e Domus

LAZIO €€

9 MAP P46, B1

Staffed by young graduates from a local *scuola alberghiera* (catering college), this luminous modern restaurant is the best option in the touristy Forum area. With minimal decor and large windows overlooking the Colonna Traiana, it's a relaxed spot to sit down to rustic local staples, all made with locally sourced ingredients, and a glass or two of regional wine. (06 6994 0273; Via Foro Traiano 82-4; meals €30-40; 9am-midnight Mon & Wed-Sat, from 10am Sun; Via dei Fori Imperiali)

47 Circus Roof Garden

RISTORANTE €€€

10 MAP P46, A4

With the Aventino hill rising in the background, the rooftop restaurant of the Forty Seven Hotel sets a romantic scene for contemporary Mediterranean cuisine. Seafood features heavily on the seasonal menu, appearing in creative antipasti, with pasta and in main courses. (06 678 78 16; www.47circusroofgarden.com; Forty Seven Hotel, Via Petroselli 47; meals €65; 12.30-3.30pm & 7pm-10.30pm; Via Petroselli)

Drinking

Terrazza Caffarelli

CAFE

11 MAP P46, A3

The Capitoline Museums' (p47) terrace cafe is a memorable place to relax over a sunset drink and swoon over magical views of the city's domes and rooftops. It also does snacks and simple meals but it's the panoramas that you'll remember here. You don't need a museum ticket to reach the 2nd-floor cafe which can be accessed from Piazzale Caffarelli. (Caffetteria dei Musei Capitolini; 06 6919 0564; Piazzale Caffarelli 4; 9.30am-7pm; Piazza Venezia)

Explore

Centro Storico

A tightly packed tangle of cobbled alleyways, Renaissance palaces, ancient ruins and baroque piazzas, the historic centre is the Rome many come to see. Its theatrical streets teem with boutiques, cafes, trattorias and stylish bars, while market traders and street artists work its vibrant squares. You'll also find a host of monuments, museums and churches, many laden with priceless artworks.

The Short List

- ***Pantheon (p54)*** *Stepping into this ancient temple and feeling the same sense of awe that the ancients must have felt 2000 years ago.*
- ***Piazza Navona (p62)*** *Admiring the beauty of this baroque piazza with its flamboyant fountains and elegant* chiesa.
- ***Galleria Doria Pamphilj (p64)*** *Browsing the artistic treasures at this fabulous private gallery.*
- ***Chiesa di San Luigi dei Francesi (p63)*** *Clocking three Caravaggio masterpieces at this historic church.*
- ***Historic Streets (p62)*** *Strolling the area's atmospheric lanes, taking in the colourful street life and hidden nooks.*

Getting There & Around

🚌 A whole fleet serves the area from Termini, including 40 and 64, which both stop at Largo di Torre Argentina and continue down Corso Vittorio Emanuele II.

Ⓜ The neighbourhood is walk-able from Barberini, Spagna and Flaminio stations, all on line A.

🚋 Tram 8 runs from Piazza Venezia to Trastevere.

Centro Storico Map on p60

Piazza Navona (p62)

Top Experience

Gaze in wonder at the Pantheon

A striking 2000-year-old temple, now a church, this is Rome's best-preserved ancient monument and one of the most influential buildings in the Western world. The greying, pockmarked exterior might look its age, but inside it's a different story; it's a unique and exhilarating experience to pass through those vast bronze doors and gaze up at the largest unreinforced concrete dome ever built.

MAP P60, D3

www.pantheonroma.com

Piazza della Rotonda

admission free

8.30am-7.30pm Mon-Sat, 9am-6pm Sun

Largo di Torre Argentina

History

In its current form the Pantheon dates to around AD 125. It was built by the emperor Hadrian over an earlier temple constructed by Marcus Agrippa in 27 BC. Hadrian's temple was dedicated to the classical gods – hence the name Pantheon, a derivation of the Greek words *pan* (all) and *theos* (god) – but in AD 608 it was consecrated as a Christian church and it's now officially known as the Basilica di Santa Maria ad Martyres.

Exterior

The monumental entrance portico consists of 16 11.8m-high columns supporting a triangular pediment. Behind the columns, two 20-tonne bronze doors – 16th-century restorations of the originals – give onto the central rotunda.

Interior

With light streaming in through the oculus (the 8.7m-diameter hole in the dome), the cylindrical marble-clad interior seems vast. Opposite the entrance is the church's main altar, while to the left are the tombs of the artist Raphael, King Umberto I and Margherita of Savoy. Over on the opposite side of the rotunda is the tomb of King Vittorio Emanuele II.

The Dome

The Pantheon's dome, considered the Romans' greatest architectural achievement, was the largest dome in the world until the 15th century when Brunelleschi beat it with his Florentine cupola. Its harmonious appearance is due to a precisely calibrated symmetry – its diameter is equal to the building's interior height of 43.4m. At its centre, the oculus plays a vital structural role by absorbing and redistributing the structure's huge tensile forces.

★ Top Tips

- The Pantheon is a working church and mass is celebrated at 5pm on Saturday and 10.30am on Sunday.
- Visit around midday to see a beam of sunlight stream in through the oculus.
- Look down as well as up – the sloping marble floor has 22 almost-invisible holes to drain away the rain that gets in through the oculus.
- Return after dark for amazing views of the building set against the ink-blue night sky.
- Audio guides are available inside for €6.

✕ Take a Break

The streets around the Pantheon are thick with trattorias, cafes and bars. For an uplifting espresso, try the nearby La Casa del Caffè Tazza d'Oro (p69), one of Rome's finest coffee houses.

Walking Tour

Piazzas of Rome

Rome's tightly packed historic centre is home to some of the city's most celebrated piazzas, and several beautiful but lesser known squares. Each has its own character but together they encapsulate much of the city's beauty, history and drama. Take this tour to discover the best of them and enjoy the area's vibrant street life.

Walk Facts

Start Largo di Torre Argentina; bus Largo di Torre Argentina

End Piazza Farnese; bus Corso Vittorio Emanuele II

Length 1.5km; three hours

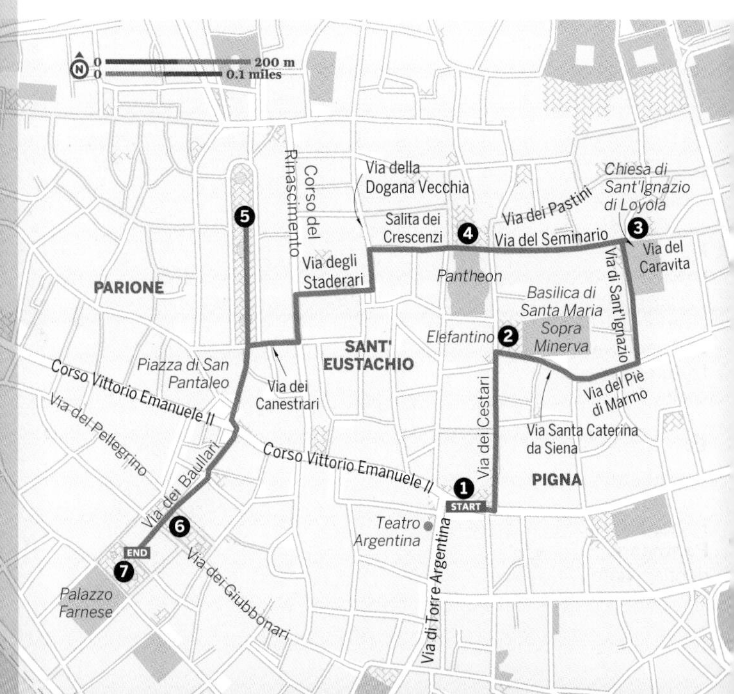

❶ Largo di Torre Argentina

Start off in Largo di Torre Argentina, set around the ruins of four Republic-era temples. On the piazza's western flank, the **Teatro Argentina** (p70), Rome's premier theatre, sits near the site where Julius Caesar was assassinated.

❷ Piazza della Minerva

Head along Via dei Cestari until you come to Piazza della Minerva and the **Elefantino**, a sculpture of a puzzled elephant carrying an Egyptian obelisk. Flanking the square, the Gothic **Basilica di Santa Maria Sopra Minerva** (p63) holds Renaissance frescoes and a minor Michelangelo.

❸ Piazza di Sant'Ignazio Loyola

Strike off down Via Santa Caterina da Siena, then take Via del Piè di Marmo and Via di Sant'Ignazio to reach the exquisite 18th-century Piazza di Sant'Ignazio Loyola. Overlooking the piazza, the **Chiesa di Sant'Ignazio di Loyola** (p63) features a magical trompe l'œil ceiling fresco.

❹ Piazza della Rotonda

A short stroll down Via del Seminario brings you to the bustling Piazza della Rotonda, where the **Pantheon** (p54) needs no introduction. Rome's best-preserved ancient building is one of the city's iconic sights with, its epic portico and dome.

❺ Piazza Navona

From the Pantheon, follow the signs to **Piazza Navona** (p62), central Rome's great showpiece square. Here, among the street artists, tourists and pigeons, you can compare the two giants of Roman baroque – Gian Lorenzo Bernini, creator of the Fontana dei Quattro Fiumi, and Francesco Borromini, author of the Chiesa di Sant'Agnese in Agone.

❻ Campo de' Fiori

On the other side of Corso Vittorio Emanuele II, the busy road that bisects the *centro storico* (historic centre), life is focused on **Campo de' Fiori** (p69). By day this noisy square stages a colourful market at night it plays host to a raucous drinking scene.

❼ Piazza Farnese

Just beyond the Campo, Piazza Farnese is a refined square overlooked by the Renaissance **Palazzo Farnese** (p65). This magnificent *palazzo*, now home to the French embassy, displays some superb frescoes, said by some to rival those of the Sistine Chapel.

Walking Tour

A Day Out in the Centro Storico

Rome's historic centre casts a powerful spell. But it's not just visitors who fall for its romantic piazzas, suggestive lanes, and streetside cafes. Away from the tourist spotlight, locals love to spend time here, shopping, unwinding over a drink, taking in an exhibition or simply hanging out with friends.

Walk Facts

Start Chiostro del Bramante; bus Corso del Rinascimento

End Rimessa Roscioli; bus Lungotevere dei Tebaldi

Length 1.8km; four hours

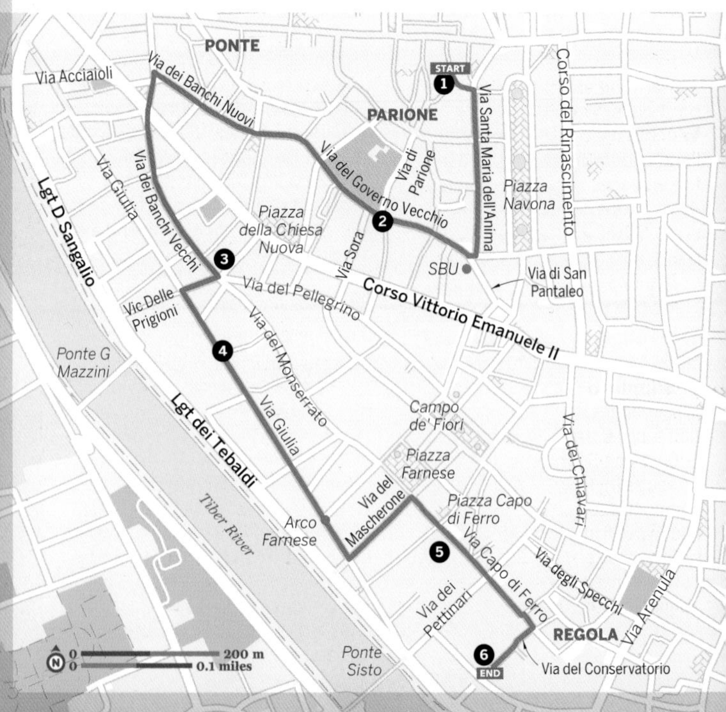

❶ Exhibition at the Chiostro del Bramante

A masterpiece of High Renaissance architectural styling, the **Chiostro del Bramante** (www.chiostrodelbramante.it; Via Arco della Pace 5; exhibitions adult/reduced €14/12; ⌚church 9.30am-6.30pm, cloister 10am-8pm Mon-Fri, to 9pm Sat & Sun; 🚌Corso del Rinascimento) provides a stunning setting for modern-art exhibitions. Afterwards, pop upstairs for a coffee, light lunch or drink at the smart in-house cafe.

❷ Shopping around Via del Governo Vecchio

A charming street lined with indie boutiques, **Via del Governo Vecchio** (🚌Corso Vittorio Emanuele II) can get touristy but locals love the vibe too; the area has some great shops, including hip jeans store **SBU** (☎06 6880 2547; www.sbu.it; Via di San Pantaleo 68-69; ⌚10am-7.30pm Mon-Sat, noon-7pm Sun; 🚌Corso Vittorio Emanuele II).

❸ Street Food at Supplizio

At **Supplizio** (☎06 8987 1920; www.supplizioroma.it; Via dei Banchi Vecchi 143; supplì €3-7; ⌚noon-3.30pm & 5-10pm Mon-Sat; 🚌Corso Vittorio Emanuele II), Rome's favourite snack, the *supplì* (a risotto ball filled with tomato sauce and stringy molten mozzarella), gets a gourmet makeover with predictably delicious results.

❹ Stroll Via Giulia

Lined with Renaissance *palazzi* and discreet fashion boutiques, **Via Giulia** (🚌Lungotevere dei Tebaldi) is a picture-perfect strip to stroll. At its southern end, the overhead **Arco Farnese** (Via Giulia; 🚌Via Giulia) was part of an ambitious, unfinished project to link two Farnese palaces.

❺ Optical Illusion at Palazzo Spada

Palazzo Spada (Palazzo Capodiferro; ☎06 683 24 09; www.galleriaspada.beniculturali.it; Piazza Capo Di Ferro 13; adult/reduced €5/2.50; ⌚8.30am-7.30pm Wed-Mon; 🚌Corso Vittorio Emanuele II) is home to a celebrated optical illusion – the Prospettiva (Perspective) – created by baroque architect Francesco Borromini. What appears to be a 25m-long corridor leading to a life-sized statue is, in fact, only 10m long, and the sculpture is only hip-height.

❻ Wine Tasting at Rimessa Roscioli

Rimessa Roscioli (☎06 6880 3914; www.winetastingrome.com; Via del Conservatorio 58; ⌚6.30-11.30pm Mon-Fri, noon-3pm & 6.30-11.30pm Sat & Sun; 📶; 🚌Lungotevere dei Tebaldi) is heaven-made for wine lovers. Exquisite dinners offer the chance to pair stellar wines with wonderful food (€33 to €65 for wine-tasting menus) or there's a Tasting Bar option, where a sommelier tailors a tasting to your budget and preferences.

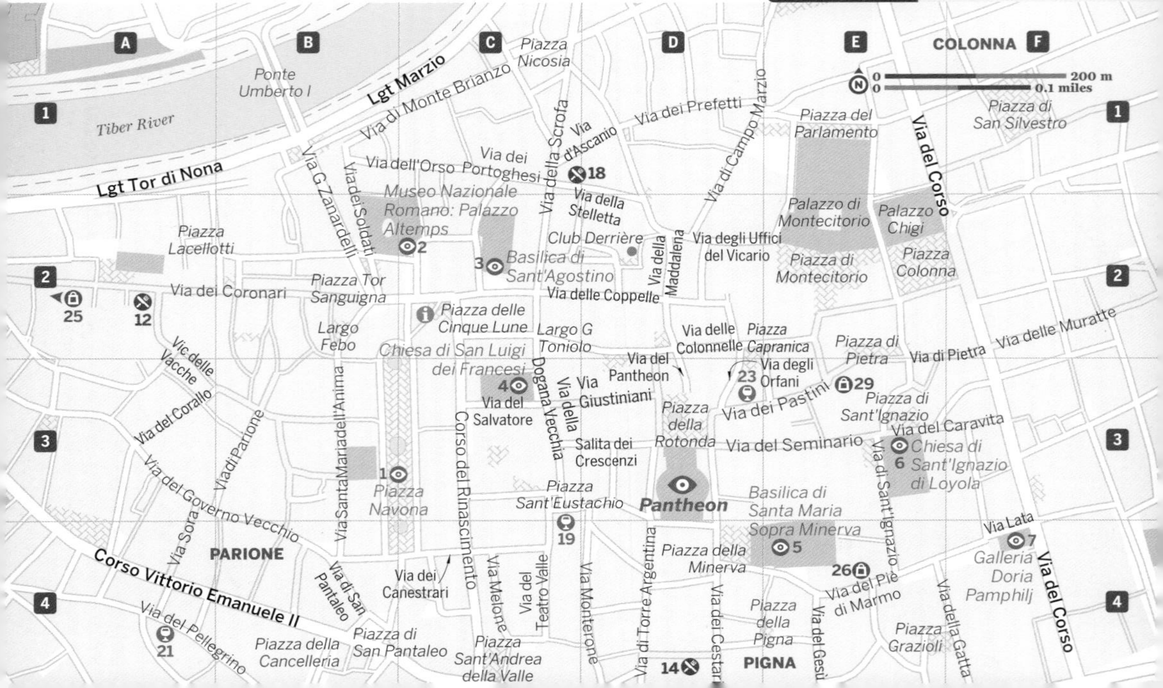

A
B
C
D
E
F
1
2
3
4
COLONNA
0 200 m
0 0.1 miles
Piazza di San Silvestro
Piazza del Parlamento
Via del Corso
Tiber River
Ponte Umberto I
Lgt Marzio
Via di Monte Brianzo
Piazza Nicosia
Lgt Tor di Nona
Via dei Prefetti
Via di Campo Marzio
Via d'Ascanio
Via della Scrofa
Via dei Portoghesi
Via dell'Orso
18
Via della Stelletta
Via G Zanardelli
Via dei Soldati
Museo Nazionale Romano: Palazzo Altemps
2
Palazzo di Montecitorio
Palazzo Chigi
Piazza Lacellotti
Club Derrière
Via della Maddalena
Via degli Uffici del Vicario
Piazza di Montecitorio
Piazza Colonna
3
Basilica di Sant'Agostino
Piazza Tor Sanguigna
Via dei Coronari
25
12
Via delle Coppelle
Piazza delle Cinque Lune
Largo Febo
Largo G Toniolo
Via delle Colonnelle
Piazza Capranica
Piazza di Pietra
Via di Pietra
Via delle Muratte
Chiesa di San Luigi dei Francesi
Vic delle Vacche
Via del Pantheon
Via degli Orfani
23
29
4
Via del Salvatore
Dogana Vecchia
Via della
Via Giustiniani
Via dei Pastini
Piazza di Sant'Ignazio
Via del Caravita
Via del Corallo
Via di Parione
Corso del Rinascimento
Piazza della Rotonda
Via del Seminario
Via Santa Maria dell'Anima
Salita dei Crescenzi
Chiesa di Sant'Ignazio di Loyola
6
Via di Sant'Ignazio
1
Piazza Navona
Piazza Sant'Eustachio
Pantheon
Basilica di Santa Maria Sopra Minerva
Via del Governo Vecchio
19
Via Lata
7
Via Sora
PARIONE
Piazza della Minerva
5
Galleria Doria Pamphilj
Corso Vittorio Emanuele II
Via di San Pantaleo
Via dei Canestrari
Via Melone
Via del Teatro Valle
Via Monterone
Via di Torre Argentina
Via dei Cestari
26
Via del Piè di Marmo
Via della Gatta
Piazza della Pigna
Via del Gesù
Piazza Grazioli
Via del Pellegrino
21
Piazza della Cancelleria
Piazza di San Pantaleo
Piazza Sant'Andrea della Valle
14
PIGNA

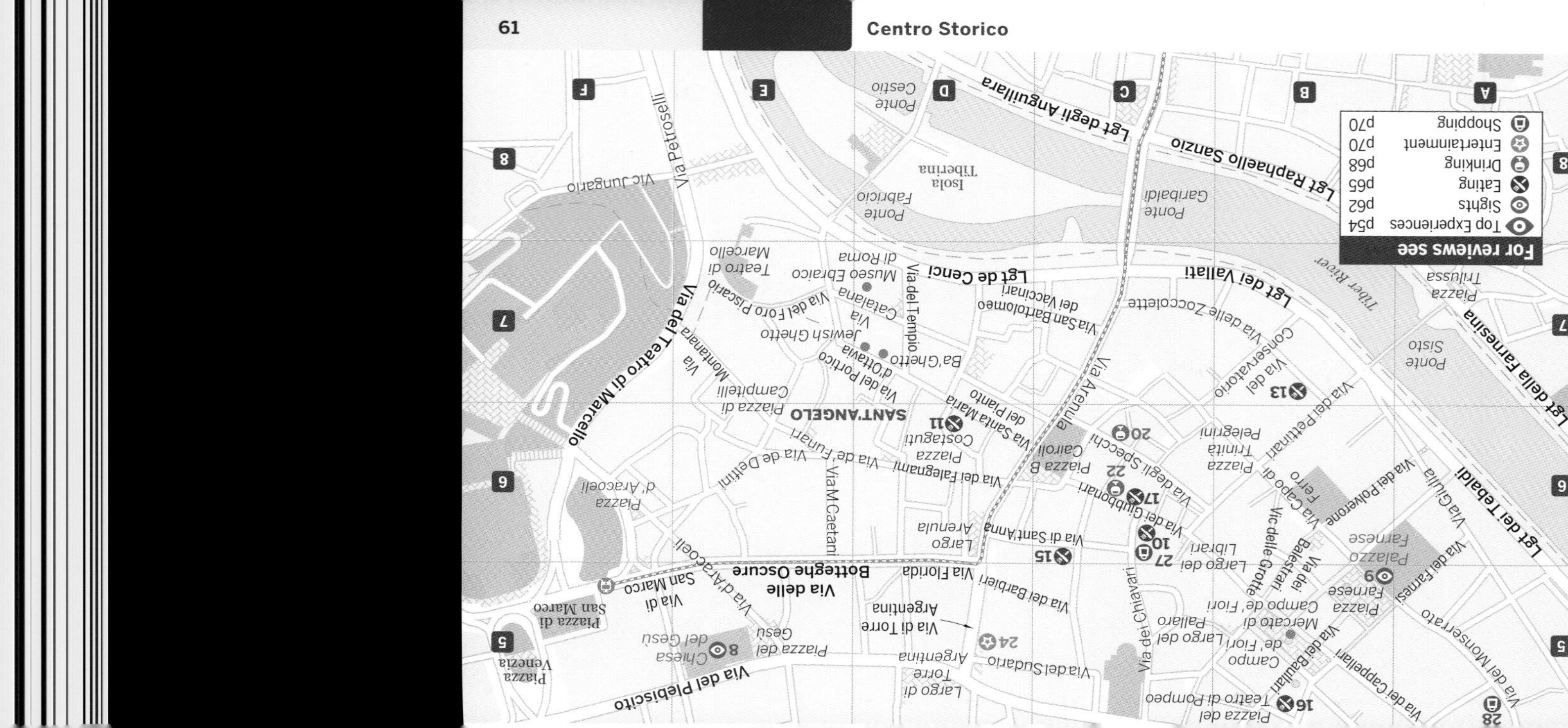
For reviews see
Top Experiences p54
Sights p62
Eating p65
Drinking p68
Entertainment p70
Shopping p70
Via del Plebiscito
Piazza Venezia
Piazza di San Marco
Via di San Marco
Chiesa del Gesù
Piazza del Gesù
Via d'Aracoeli
Piazza d' Aracoeli
Via delle Botteghe Oscure
Via M Caetani
Via de' Delfini
Via de' Funari
Via dei Falegnami
Piazza di Campitelli
Via Montanara
Via del Teatro di Marcello
Via Petroselli
Vic Jungario
SANT'ANGELO
Piazza Costaguti
Via del Portico d'Ottavia
Ba'Ghetto
Jewish Ghetto
Via Catalana
Via del Foro Piscario
Teatro di Marcello
Museo Ebraico di Roma
Via del Tempio
Lgt de Cenci
Ponte Fabricio
Isola Tiberina
Ponte Cestio
Lgt degli Anguillara
Largo di Torre Argentina
Via di Torre Argentina
Via Florida
Largo Arenula
Via di Sant'Anna
Via dei Barbieri
Via del Sudario
Via Santa Maria del Pianto
Piazza B Cairoli
Via Arenula
Via San Bartolomeo dei Vaccinari
Via dei Chiavari
Via dei Giubbonari
Via degli Specchi
Largo del Pallaro
Largo dei Librari
Piazza del Teatro di Pompeo
Campo de' Fiori
Mercato di Campo de' Fiori
Via dei Baullari
Via dei Cappellari
Via del Monserrato
Via dei Farnesi
Piazza Farnese
Palazzo Farnese
Via dei Balestrari
Vic delle Grotte
Via Capo di Ferro
Piazza Trinità Pelegrini
Via dei Polverone
Via Giulia
Via dei Pettinari
Via del Conservatorio
Via delle Zoccolette
Lgt dei Vallati
Ponte Garibaldi
Lgt Raphaello Sanzio
Lgt dei Tebaldi
Lgt della Farnesina
Ponte Sisto
Piazza Trilussa
Tiber River

Sights

Piazza Navona

PIAZZA

1 MAP P60, B3

With its showy fountains, baroque *palazzi* and colourful cast of street artists, hawkers and tourists, Piazza Navona is central Rome's elegant showcase square. Built over the 1st-century **Stadio di Domiziano** (Domitian's Stadium; 06 6880 5311; www.stadiodomiziano.com; Via di Tor Sanguigna 3; adult/reduced €8/6; 10am-6.30pm Sun-Fri, to 7.30pm Sat), it was paved over in the 15th century and for almost 300 years hosted the city's main market. Its grand centrepiece is Bernini's **Fontana dei Quattro Fiumi** (Fountain of the Four Rivers), a flamboyant fountain featuring an Egyptian obelisk and muscular personifications of the rivers Nile, Ganges, Danube and Plate. (Corso del Rinascimento)

Museo Nazionale Romano: Palazzo Altemps

MUSEUM

2 MAP P60, C2

Just north of Piazza Navona, Palazzo Altemps is a beautiful late-15th-century *palazzo,* housing the best of the Museo Nazionale Romano's formidable collection of classical sculpture. Many pieces come from the celebrated Ludovisi collection, amassed by Cardinal Ludovico Ludovisi in the 17th century. (06 68 48 51; www.museonazionaleromano.beniculturali.it; Piazza Sant'Apollinare 46; adult/

Museo Nazionale Romano: Palazzo Altemps

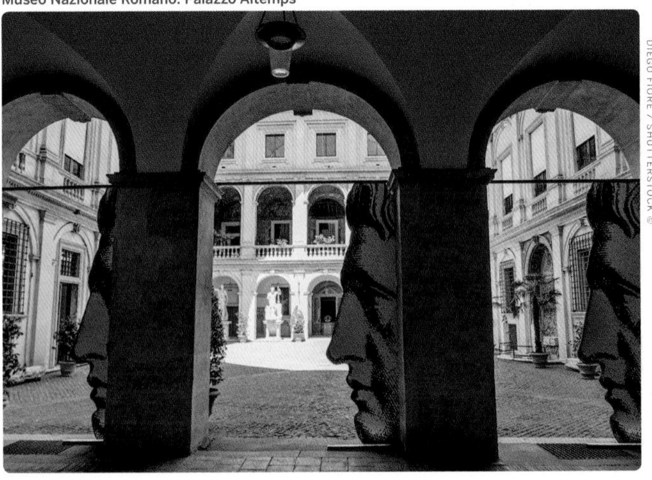

reduced €10/5, incl Palazzo Massimo alle Terme, Crypta Balbi & Terme di Diocleziano €12/6; 9am-7.45pm Tue-Sun; Corso del Rinascimento)

Basilica di Sant'Agostino

BASILICA

3 MAP P60, C2

The plain white facade of this early Renaissance church, built in the 15th century and renovated in the late 1700s, gives no indication of the impressive art inside. The most famous work is Caravaggio's *Madonna dei Pellegrini* (Madonna of the Pilgrims), in the first chapel on the left, but you'll also find a fresco by Raphael and a much-venerated sculpture by Jacopo Sansovino. (06 6880 1962; Piazza di Sant'Agostino 80; 7.45am-noon & 4-7.30pm; Corso del Rinascimento)

Chiesa di San Luigi dei Francesi

CHURCH

4 MAP P60, C3

Church to Rome's French community since 1589, this opulent baroque *chiesa* is home to a celebrated trio of Caravaggio paintings: the *Vocazione di San Matteo* (The Calling of Saint Matthew), the *Martirio di San Matteo* (The Martyrdom of Saint Matthew) and *San Matteo e l'angelo* (Saint Matthew and the Angel), known collectively as the St Matthew cycle. (06 68 82 71; Piazza di San Luigi dei Francesi 5; 9.30am-12.45pm & 2.30-6.30pm Mon-Fri, 9.30am-12.15pm & 2.30-6.45pm Sat, 11.30am-12.45pm & 2.30-6.45pm Sun; Corso del Rinascimento)

Basilica di Santa Maria Sopra Minerva

BASILICA

5 MAP P60, E4

Built on the site of three pagan temples, including one dedicated to the goddess Minerva, the Dominican Basilica di Santa Maria Sopra Minerva is Rome's only Gothic church. However, little remains of the original 13th-century structure and these days the main drawcard is a minor Michelangelo sculpture and the magisterial, art-rich interior. (www.santamariasopraminerva.it; Piazza della Minerva 42; 6.55am-7pm Mon-Fri, 10am-12.30pm & 3.30-7pm Sat, 8.10am-12.30pm & 3.30-7pm Sun; Largo di Torre Argentina)

Chiesa di Sant'Ignazio di Loyola

CHURCH

6 MAP P60, E3

Flanking a delightful rococo piazza, this important Jesuit church features a Carlo Maderno facade and two celebrated trompe l'œil frescoes by Andrea Pozzo (1642–1709). One cleverly depicts a fake dome, while the other, on the nave ceiling, shows St Ignatius Loyola being welcomed into paradise by Christ and the Madonna. (06 679 44 06; https://santignazio.gesuiti.it; Piazza di Sant'Ignazio; 7.30am-7pm Mon-Sat, from 9am Sun; Via del Corso)

Rome's Architectural Timeline

c 4th century BC–AD 5th century The ancient Romans make huge advances in engineering techniques, constructing monumental public buildings, bridges, aqueducts, housing blocks and an underground sewerage system.

4th–12th centuries Church building is the focus of architectural activity in the Middle Ages as Rome's early Christian leaders seek to stamp their authority on the city.

15th–16th centuries Based on humanism and a reappraisal of classical precepts, the Renaissance hits an all-time high in the first two decades of the 16th century, a period known as the High Renaissance.

17th century Developing out of the Counter-Reformation, the baroque flourishes in Rome, fuelled by Church money and the genius of Gian Lorenzo Bernini and his hated rival Francesco Borromini.

18th century A short-lived but theatrical style born out of the baroque, the florid rococo gifts Rome some of its most popular sights.

late 18th century–early 19th century Piazza del Popolo takes on its current form courtesy of Rome's top neoclassical architect, Giuseppe Valadier.

late 19th century Rome gets a major post-unification makeover – roads are built, piazzas are laid and residential quarters spring up to house government bureaucrats.

early 20th century Muscular and modern, Italian rationalism plays to Mussolini's vision of a fearless, futuristic Rome, a 20th-century *caput mundi* (world capital).

1990s–present Rome provides the historic stage upon which some of the world's top contemporary architects experiment. Criticism and praise are meted out in almost equal measure.

Galleria Doria Pamphilj GALLERY

7 MAP P60, F4

Hidden behind the grimy grey exterior of Palazzo Doria Pamphilj, this wonderful gallery holds one of Rome's richest private art collections, with works by Raphael, Tintoretto, Titian, Caravaggio, Bernini and Velázquez, as well as several Flemish masters. Masterpieces abound, but the undisputed star is Velázquez' portrait of an implacable Pope Innocent X, who grumbled that the depiction was 'too real'. For a comparison, check out Gian Lorenzo Bernini's sculptural interpretation of the same subject. (☎06 679 73 23; www.doriapamphilj.it; Via del Corso 305; adult/reduced €12/8; ⌚9am-7pm, last entry 6pm; 🚌Via del Corso)

Chiesa del Gesù CHURCH

8 ◉ MAP P60, E5

An imposing example of Counter-Reformation architecture, Rome's most important Jesuit church is a fabulous treasure trove of baroque art. Headline works include a swirling vault fresco by Giovanni Battista Gaulli (aka Il Baciccia) and Andrea del Pozzo's opulent tomb for Ignatius Loyola, the Spanish soldier and saint who founded the Jesuits in 1540. St Ignatius lived in the church from 1544 until his death in 1556 and you can visit his private rooms to the right of the main church. (☎06 69 70 01; www.chiesadelgesu.org; Piazza del Gesù; ⌚6.45am-12.45pm & 4-7.30pm, St Ignatius rooms 4-6pm Mon-Sat, 10am-noon Sun; 🚌Largo di Torre Argentina)

Palazzo Farnese HISTORIC BUILDING

9 ◉ MAP P60, B5

Home to the French embassy, this towering Renaissance *palazzo*, one of Rome's finest, was started in 1514 by Antonio da Sangallo the Younger, continued by Michelangelo and finished by Giacomo della Porta. Inside, there are frescoes by Annibale and Agostino Carracci that are said by some to rival Michelangelo's in the Sistine Chapel. The highlight, painted between 1597 and 1608, is the monumental ceiling fresco *Amori degli Dei* (The Loves of the Gods) in the Galleria dei Carracci. (www.inventerrome.com; Piazza Farnese; tours €9; ⌚guided tours 3pm, 4pm & 5pm Mon, Wed & Fri; 🚌Corso Vittorio Emanuele II)

Eating

Forno Roscioli BAKERY €

10 MAP P60, C6

This is one of Rome's top bakeries, much loved by lunching locals who crowd here for luscious sliced pizza, prize pastries and hunger-sating *supplì* (risotto balls). The pizza margherita is superb, if messy to eat, and there's also a counter serving hot pastas and vegetable side dishes. (☎06 686 40 45; www.anticofornoroscioli.it; Via dei Chiavari 34; pizza slices from €2, snacks €2.50; ⌚7am-8pm Mon-Sat, 8.30am-7pm Sun; 🚋Via Arenula)

Antico Forno Urbani BAKERY €

11 MAP P60, D6

This Ghetto kosher bakery makes some of the best *pizza al taglio* (sliced pizza) in town. It can get extremely busy but once you catch a whiff of the yeasty smell it's impossible to resist a quick stop. Everything's good, including its fabulous *pizza con patate* (pizza topped with thin slices of potato). (☎06 689 32 35; Piazza

Jewish Ghetto in Rome

Centred on lively Via del Portico d'Ottavia, the **Jewish Ghetto** (Map p60, D7; Lungotevere de' Cenci) is an atmospheric area studded with artisans' studios, small shops, kosher bakeries and popular trattorias. Crowning everything is the distinctive square dome of Rome's main **synagogue** (Jewish Museum of Rome; Map p60, D7; 06 6840 0661; www.museoebraico.roma.it; Via Catalana; adult/reduced €11/8; 10am-5.15pm Sun-Thu, to 3.15pm Fri summer, 9.30am-4.30pm Sun-Thu, 9am-2pm Fri winter; Lungotevere de' Cenci).

Rome's Jewish community dates back to the 2nd century BC, making it one of the oldest in Europe. Confinement to the Ghetto came in 1555 when Pope Paul IV ushered in a period of official intolerance that lasted, on and off, until the 20th century. Ironically, though, confinement meant that the Jewish cultural and religious identity survived intact.

Roman-Jewish cuisine is deeply entrenched in Rome's culinary make-up and there's nowhere better to experience it than the Ghetto. For a taste, try **Ba'Ghetto** (Map p60, D7; 06 6889 2868; www.baghetto.com; Via del Portico d'Ottavia 57; meals €30-35; noon-11.30pm Mon-Thu & Sun, to 3pm Fri, 6-11.30pm Sat; Via Arenula), a long-standing neighbourhood restaurant that serves kosher food and local staples such as *carciofo alla guidia* (crisp fried artichoke).

Costaguti 31; pizza slices from €1.50; 7.40am-2.30pm & 5-7.45pm Mon-Fri, 8.30am-1.30pm Sat, 9.30am-1pm Sun; Via Arenula)

Gelateria del Teatro GELATO €

12 MAP P60, A2

All the gelato served at this excellent gelateria is prepared on site – look through the window and you'll see how. There are numerous flavours, all made from premium seasonal ingredients, ranging from evergreen favourites such as pistachio and hazelnut to inventive creations like rosemary, honey and lemon. (06 4547 4880; www.gelateriadelteatro.it; Via dei Coronari 65; gelato from €3; 11am-8pm winter, 10am-10.30pm summer; Via Zanardelli)

Pianostrada RISTORANTE €€

13 MAP P60, B7

This uberhip bistro-restaurant, in a white space with vintage furnishings and a glorious summer courtyard, is a must. Reserve ahead, or settle for a stool at the bar and enjoy views of the kitchen at work. The cuisine is creative, seasonal and veg-packed, including gourmet open sandwiches and sensational focaccia, as well as full-blown mains. (☎06 8957 2296; www.facebook.com/pianostrada; Via delle Zoccolette 22; meals €40-45; ⏰1-4pm & 7pm-midnight Tue-Fri, 10am-midnight Sat & Sun; 🚋Via Arenula)

La Ciambella

ITALIAN €€

14 MAP P60, D4

Near the Pantheon but as yet largely undiscovered by the tourist hordes, this friendly restaurant beats much of the neighbourhood competition. Its handsome, light-filled interior is set over the ruins of the Terme di Agrippa, visible through transparent floor panels, setting an attractive stage for interesting, imaginative food. (☎06 683 29 30; www.la-ciambella.it; Via dell'Arco della Ciambella 20; meals €35-45; ⏰noon-11pm Tue-Sun; 🚌Largo di Torre Argentina)

Emma Pizzeria

PIZZA €€

15 MAP P60, C6

Tucked in behind the Chiesa di San Carlo ai Catinari, Emma is a stylish set-up with outdoor seating and a spacious, art-clad interior. It specialises in cracking wood-fired pizzas, ranging from the ever-present margherita to more inventive choices topped with guest ingredients such as Spanish *pata negra* ham and Cantabrian anchovies. Alternatively, go for a classic Roman pasta dish. (☎06 6476 0475; www.emmapizzeria.com; Via del Monte della Farina 28-29; pizzas €8-18, meals €35; ⏰12.30-3pm & 7-11.30pm; 🚋Via Arenula)

Grappolo D'Oro

TRATTORIA €€

16 MAP P60, B5

This welcoming modern trattoria stands out among the many lacklustre options around Campo de' Fiori. The emphasis is on updated regional cuisine, so look out for dishes such as pasta with anchovies, pecorino and cherry tomatoes, and rich desserts like *zabaglione* spiked with fortified Marsala wine. (☎06 689 70 80; www.hosteriagrappolodoro.it; Piazza della Cancelleria 80; meals €35; ⏰12.30-3pm & 6.30-11pm, closed Wed lunch; 🚌Corso Vittorio Emanuele II)

Salumeria Roscioli

RISTORANTE €€€

17 MAP P60, C6

The name Roscioli has long been a byword for foodie excellence in Rome, and this deli-restaurant is the place to experience it. Tables are set alongside the counter, laden with mouth-watering Italian and foreign delicacies, and in a small bottle-lined space behind. The food, including traditional Roman pastas, is top notch and there are some truly outstanding wines. Reservations essential. (☎06 687 52 87; www.salumeriaroscioli.com; Via dei Giubbonari 21; meals €55; ⏰12.30-4pm & 7pm-midnight Mon-Sat; 🚋Via Arenula)

Retrobottega

RISTORANTE €€€

18 MAP P60, C1

Fine dining goes casual at trendy Retrobottega. Here you'll

be sitting on a stool at a high communal table or chatting with the chef as he plates dishes at the counter. The food, in keeping with the experimental vibe and contemporary decor, is original and creative Italian. (06 6813 6310; www.retro-bottega.com; Via della Stelletta 4; à la carte meals €45, 4-/7-course menus €55/75; 6.30-11.30pm Mon, from noon Tue-Sun; Corso del Rinascimento)

Drinking

Caffè Sant'Eustachio COFFEE

19 MAP P60, C4

Always busy, this workaday cafe near the Pantheon is reckoned by many to serve the best coffee in town. To make it, the bartenders sneakily beat the first drops of an espresso with several teaspoons of sugar to create a frothy paste to which they add the rest of the coffee. The result is superbly smooth. (06 6880 2048; www.santeustachioilcaffe.it; Piazza Sant'Eustachio 82; 7.30am-1am Sun-Thu, to 1.30am Fri, to 2am Sat; Corso del Rinascimento)

Open Baladin CRAFT BEER

20 MAP P60, C6

This modern pub near Campo de' Fiori has long been a leading light in Rome's craft-beer scene, and with more than 40 beers on tap and up to 100 bottled brews (many from Italian artisanal microbreweries) it's a top place for a pint. As well as great beer, expect a laid-back vibe and a young, international crowd. (06

Caffè Sant'Eustachio

DIEGO FIORE / SHUTTERSTOCK ©

683 89 89; www.openbaladinroma.it; Via degli Specchi 6; noon-2am; ; Via Arenula)

Barnum Cafe

CAFE

21 MAP P60, A4

A laid-back *Friends*-style cafe, evergreen Barnum is the sort of place you could quickly get used to. With its shabby-chic furniture and white bare-brick walls, it's a relaxed spot for a breakfast cappuccino, a light lunch or a late-afternoon drink. Come evening, a coolly dressed-down crowd gathers to sip expertly mixed craft cocktails. (06 6476 0483; www.barnumcafe.com; Via del Pellegrino 87; 9am-10pm Mon, 8.30am-2am Tue-Sat; ; Corso Vittorio Emanuele II)

Roscioli Caffè

CAFE

22 MAP P60, C6

In Rome, the Roscioli name is a guarantee of good things to come: the family runs one of Rome's most celebrated delis (p67) and a hugely popular bakery (p65), and this cafe doesn't disappoint, either. The coffee is luxurious and the artfully crafted pastries, petits fours and *panini* taste as good as they look. (06 8916 5330; www.rosciolicaffe.com; Piazza Benedetto Cairoli 16; 7am-11pm Mon-Sat, 8am-6pm Sun, closed mid-Aug; Via Arenula)

Campo de' Fiori

Colourful and always busy, **Campo de' Fiori** is a major focus of Roman life: by day it hosts one of the city's best-known **markets** (Map p60, B5; Campo de' Fiori; 7am-2pm Mon-Sat; Corso Vittorio Emanuele II); by night it heaves with tourists and young drinkers who spill out of its many bars and restaurants. For centuries the square was the site of public executions. It was here that philosopher Giordano Bruno was burned for heresy in 1600, hence the sinister statue of the hooded monk, created by Ettore Ferrari in 1889.

La Casa del Caffè Tazza d'Oro

COFFEE

23 MAP P60, D3

A busy cafe with burnished 1940s fittings, this is one of Rome's best coffee houses. Its position near the Pantheon makes it touristy but its coffees are brilliant – the espresso hits the mark every time and there's a range of delicious *caffè* concoctions, including *granita di caffè*, a crushed-ice coffee served with whipped cream. (06 678 97 92; www.tazzadorocoffeeshop.com; Via degli Orfani 84-86; 7am-8pm Mon-Sat, 10.30am-7.30pm Sun; Via del Corso)

Speakeasy Cocktails

Found in the back room of an unassuming trattoria (Osteria delle Coppelle), **Club Derrière** (Map p60, D2; 393 5661077; www.facebook.com/clubderriere roma; Vicolo delle Coppelle 59; 10pm-4am; ; Corso del Rinascimento) is an enigmatic speakeasy where a suit of armour serves as unofficial bouncer. Bartenders don ties and waistcoats and sling sleek cocktails (€12) often inspired by cultural figures, such as their Edgar Allan Poe, a heady mix of sherry, Knob Creek rye, chocolate and Angostura bitters.

Entertainment

Teatro Argentina

THEATRE

24 MAP P60, D5

Founded in 1732, Rome's top theatre is one of three managed by the Teatro di Roma along with the **Teatro India** (06 8775 2210 Lungotevere Vittorio Gassman 1; Stazione Trastevere) and Teatro di Villa Torlonia. Rossini's *Barber of Seville* premiered here in 1816, and these days it stages a wide-ranging programme of classic and contemporary drama, dance and classical music. (box office 06 68400 0311; www.teatrodiroma.net; Largo di Torre Argentina 52; tickets €12-40; Largo di Torre Argentina)

Shopping

Marta Ray

SHOES

25 MAP P60, A2

Women's ballet flats and elegant, everyday bags in rainbow colours and super-soft leather are the hallmarks of the Rome-born Marta Ray brand. At this store, one of three in town, you'll find a selection of trademark flats as well as ankle boots and an attractive line in modern, beautifully designed handbags. (06 6880 2641; www.martaray.it; Via dei Coronari 121; 10am-8pm; Via Zanardelli)

Salumeria Roscioli

FOOD & DRINKS

Rome's most celebrated deli (see 17 Map p60, C6) showcases a spectacular smorgasbord of prize products ranging from cured hams and cheeses to conserves, dried pastas, olive oils, aged balsamic vinegars and wines. Alongside celebrated Italian fare you'll also find top international foodstuffs such as French cheese, Iberian ham and Scottish salmon. (06 687 52 87; www.salumeriaroscioli.com; Via dei Giubbonari 21; 8.30am-8.30pm Mon-Sat; Via Arenula)

Confetteria Moriondo & Gariglio

CHOCOLATE

26 MAP P60, E4

Roman poet Trilussa was so smitten with this chocolate shop – established by the Torinese confectioners to the royal house of Savoy – that he was moved to mention it in verse. And we agree: it's a gem. Decorated like an elegant tearoom, it specialises in handmade chocolates and confections such as marrons glacés, many prepared according to original 19th-century recipes. (06 699 08 56; Via del Piè di Marmo 21-22; 9am-7.30pm Mon-Sat; Via del Corso)

Ibiz – Artigianato in Cuoio

FASHION & ACCESSORIES

27 MAP P60, C6

In her diminutive family workshop, Elisa Nepi and her team craft beautiful butter-soft leather wallets, bags, belts, keyrings and sandals, in elegant designs and myriad colours. You can pick up a belt for about €35, while for a shoulder bag you should bank on around €145. (06 6830 7297; www.ibizroma.it; Via dei Chiavari 39; 10am-7.30pm Mon-Sat; Corso Vittorio Emanuele II)

Chez Dede

CONCEPT STORE

28 MAP P60, A5

This ultra-chic boutique offers a curated selection of handcrafted accessories, fashions, homeware and books. Particularly sought after are its signature canvas and leather tote bags but you'll also find original artworks, hand-painted ceramics and limited-edition perfumes, all displayed with effortless cool in the belle-époque-styled interior. (06 8377 2934; www.chezdede.com; Via di Monserrato 35; 3.30-7.30pm Mon, from 10.30am Tue-Sat; Lungotevere dei Tebaldi)

Bartolucci

TOYS

29 MAP P60, E3

It's difficult to resist going into this magical toyshop where everything is carved out of wood. By the main entrance, a Pinocchio pedals his bike robotically, perhaps dreaming of the full-size motorbike parked nearby, while inside there are all manner of ticking clocks, rocking horses, planes and more Pinocchios than you're likely to see in your whole life. (06 6919 0894; www.bartolucci.com; Via dei Pastini 98; 10am-10pm; Via del Corso)

Explore

Vatican City, Borgo & Prati

The Vatican, the world's smallest state, sits across the river from Rome's historic precinct. Centred on St Peter's Basilica, it holds some of Italy's most revered artworks, many housed in the vast Vatican Museums, as well as batteries of overpriced restaurants and souvenir shops. Nearby, Castel Sant'Angelo looms over the Borgo district and upscale Prati offers excellent eating and shopping.

The Short List

- ***Sistine Chapel (p78)*** *Gazing heavenwards at Michelangelo's ceiling frescoes and his terrifying Last Judgment.*
- ***St Peter's Basilica (p80)*** *Being blown away by the super-sized opulence of the Vatican's showpiece church.*
- ***Castel Sant'Angelo (p88)*** *Revelling in wonderful rooftop views from this landmark castle.*
- ***Stanze di Raffaello (p77)*** *Marvelling at Raphael's masterpiece, La Scuola di Atene, in the Vatican Museums.*

Getting There & Around

From Termini, bus 40 is the quickest one to the Vatican: bus 64 runs a similar route but stops more often. Bus 81 runs to Piazza del Risorgimento via the *centro storico* (historic centre).

M Take line A to Ottaviano-San Pietro.

Tram 19 serves Piazza del Risorgimento via San Lorenzo and Villa Borghese.

Vatican City, Borgo & Prati Map on p86

St Peter's Basilica (p80) F11PHOTO / SHUTTERSTOCK ©

Galleria delle Carte Geografiche (p77)

Top Experience

Discover a masterpiece at the Vatican Museums

Visiting the Vatican Museums is anunforgettable experience. With some 7km of exhibitions and more masterpieces than many small countries can call their own, this vast complex boasts one of the world's greatest art collections. Highlights include classical statuary in the Museo Pio-Clementino, a suite of rooms frescoed by Raphael, and the Michelangelo-decorated Sistine Chapel.

MAP P86, C3

Musei Vaticani

www.museivaticani.va

Viale Vaticano

adult/reduced €17/8

9am-6pm Mon-Sat, to 2pm last Sun of month

M Ottaviano-San Pietro

Pinacoteca

Often overlooked by visitors, the papal picture gallery displays paintings dating from the 11th to 19th centuries, with works by Giotto, Fra' Angelico, Filippo Lippi, Perugino, Titian, Guido Reni, Guercino, Pietro da Cortona, Caravaggio and Leonardo da Vinci.

Look out for a trio of paintings by Raphael in Room VIII – the *Madonna di Foligno* (Madonna of Folignano), the *Incoronazione della Vergine* (Crowning of the Virgin), and *La Trasfigurazione* (Transfiguration), which was completed by his students after his death in 1520. Other highlights include Leonardo da Vinci's haunting and unfinished *San Gerolamo* (St Jerome), and Caravaggio's *Deposizione* (Deposition from the Cross).

Museo Chiaramonti & Braccio Nuovo

This museum is effectively the long corridor that runs down the lower east side of the Palazzetto di Belvedere. Its walls are lined with thousands of statues and busts representing everything from immortal gods to playful cherubs and ugly Roman patricians.

Near the end of the hall, off to the right, is the Braccio Nuovo (New Wing), which contains a celebrated statue of the Nile as a reclining god covered by 16 babies.

Museo Pio-Clementino

This stunning museum contains some of the Vatican's finest classical statuary, including the peerless *Apollo Belvedere* and the 1st-century BC *Laocoön*, both in the **Cortile Ottagono** (Octagonal Courtyard).

Before you go into the courtyard, take a moment to admire the 1st-century *Apoxyomenos*, one of the earliest known sculptures to depict a figure with a raised arm.

★ Top Tips

- Avoid horrendous queues: book tickets (€4 fee) online (http://biglietteriamusei.vatican.va/musei/tickets/do) or at Ufficio Pellegrini e Turisti (p183).
- Last Sunday of the month the museums are free (and busy).
- Consider an audioguide (€8) or *Guide to the Vatican Museums and City* (€13).
- Minimise crowds: Tuesdays and Thursdays are quietest; Wednesday mornings are good; afternoons are better than mornings; avoid Mondays and rainy days.
- Check the website for excellent tours.
- Strollers are permitted inside.

Take a Break

There's a bistro in the Cortile della Pigna, self-service cafeterias, and a cafe near the Pinacoteca.

For a bite to remember, head to Bonci Pizzarium (p89), one of Rome's best sliced pizza joints.

To the left as you enter the courtyard, the *Apollo Belvedere* is a 2nd-century Roman copy of a 4th-century-BC Greek bronze. A beautifully proportioned representation of the sun god Apollo, it's considered one of the great masterpieces of classical sculpture. Nearby, the *Laocoön* depicts the mythical death of the Trojan priest who warned his fellow citizens not to take the wooden horse left by the Greeks.

Back inside, the **Sala degli Animali** is filled with sculpted creatures and magnificent 4th-century mosaics. Continuing on, you come to the **Sala delle Muse** (Room of the Muses), centred on the *Torso Belvedere,* another of the museum's must-sees. A fragment of a muscular 1st-century-BC Greek sculpture, this was found in Campo de' Fiori and used by Michelangelo as a model for his *ignudi* (male nudes) in the Sistine Chapel.

The next room, the **Sala Rotonda** (Round Room), contains a number of colossal statues, including a gilded-bronze *Ercole* (Hercules) and an exquisite floor mosaic. The enormous basin in the centre of the room was found at Nero's Domus Aurea and is made out of a single piece of red porphyry stone.

Museo Gregoriano Egizio

Founded by Pope Gregory XVI in 1839, this Egyptian museum displays pieces taken from Egypt in ancient Roman times.

Museo Pio-Clementino (p75)

Museo Gregoriano Etrusco

At the top of the 18th-century Simonetti staircase, this fascinating museum contains artefacts unearthed in the Etruscan tombs of northern Lazio, as well as a superb collection of vases and Roman antiquities.

Galleria dei Candelabri & Galleria degli Arazzi

The **Galleria dei Candelabri** is packed with classical sculpture and several elegantly carved candelabras that give the gallery its name. The corridor continues through to the **Galleria degli Arazzi** (Tapestry Gallery) and its huge hanging tapestries.

Galleria delle Carte Geografiche & Sala Sobieski

One of the unsung heroes of the Vatican Museums, the 120m-long Map Gallery is hung with 40 huge topographical maps. These maps were created between 1580 and 1583 for Pope Gregory XIII based on drafts by Ignazio Danti, one of the leading cartographers of his day.

Beyond the gallery, the **Sala Sobieski** is named after an enormous 19th-century painting depicting the victory of the Polish King John III Sobieski over the Turks in 1683.

Stanze di Raffaello

These four frescoed chambers, currently undergoing partial restoration, were part of Pope Julius II's private apartments. Raphael himself painted the Stanza della Segnatura (1508–11) and Stanza d'Eliodoro (1512–14), while the Stanza dell'Incendio (1514–17) and Sala di Costantino (1517–24) were decorated by students following his designs.

The first room you come to is the **Sala di Costantino**, which features a huge fresco depicting Constantine's defeat of Maxentius at the battle of Milvian Bridge.

The **Stanza d'Eliodoro**, which was used for private audiences, takes its name from the *Cacciata d'Eliodoro* (Expulsion of Heliodorus from the Temple), an allegorical work reflecting Pope Julius II's policy of forcing foreign powers off Church lands. To its right, the *Messa di Bolsena* (Mass of Bolsena) shows Julius paying homage to the relic of a 13th-century miracle at the lakeside town of Bolsena. Next is the Incontro di *Leone Magno con Attila* (Encounter of Leo the Great with Attila) by Raphael and his school and, on the fourth wall, the *Liberazione di San Pietro* (Liberation of St Peter), a brilliant work illustrating Raphael's masterful ability to depict light.

The **Stanza della Segnatura**, Julius' study and library, was the first room that Raphael painted, and it's here that you'll find his great masterpiece, *La Scuola* *di Atene* (The School of Athens), featuring philosophers and scholars gathered around Plato and Aristotle. The seated figure in front of the steps is believed to be Michelangelo, while the figure of Plato is said to be a portrait of Leonardo da Vinci, and Euclide (the bald man bending over) is Bramante. Raphael also included a self-portrait in the lower right corner – he's the second figure from the right.

The most famous work in the **Stanza dell'Incendio di Borgo** is the Incendio di Borgo (Fire in the Borgo), which depicts Pope Leo IV extinguishing a fire by making the sign of the cross. The ceiling was painted by Raphael's master, Perugino.

Sistine Chapel

The jewel in the Vatican crown, the Cappella Sistina (Sistine Chapel) is home to two of the world's most famous works of art – Michelangelo's ceiling frescoes (1508–12) and his *Giudizio Universale* (Last Judgment; 1536–41). The chapel also serves an important religious function as the place where the conclave meets to elect a new pope.

Ceiling Frescoes

The Sistine Chapel provided the greatest challenge of Michelangelo's career and painting the entire 800-sq-m ceiling at a height of more than 20m pushed him to the limits of his genius.

The focus of his design, which is best viewed from the chapel's main entrance in the east wall, are nine central panels depicting stories from the book of Genesis. Set around these are 20 athletic male nudes known as *ignudi* and a colourful cast of sibyls, prophets and biblical figures.

As you look up from the east wall, the first panel is the *Drunkenness of Noah*, followed by *The Flood*, and the *Sacrifice of Noah*. Next, *Original Sin and Banishment from the Garden of Eden* famously depicts Adam and Eve being sent packing after accepting the forbidden fruit from Satan, represented by a snake with the body of a woman coiled around a tree. The *Creation of Eve* is then followed by the *Creation of Adam*. This, one of the most famous images in Western art, shows a bearded God pointing his finger at Adam, thus bringing him to life. Completing the sequence are the *Separation of Land from Sea*; the *Creation of the Sun, Moon and Plants*; and the *Separation of Light from Darkness*, featuring a fearsome God reaching out to touch the sun.

Giudizio Universale

Michelangelo's second stint in the Sistine Chapel resulted in the Last Judgment, his highly charged depiction of Christ's second coming on the 200-sq-m western wall.

It shows Christ – in the centre near the top – passing sentence over the souls of the dead as they are torn from their graves to face him. The saved get to stay up in heaven (in the upper right), the damned are sent down to face the demons in hell (in the bottom right).

Vatican Museums

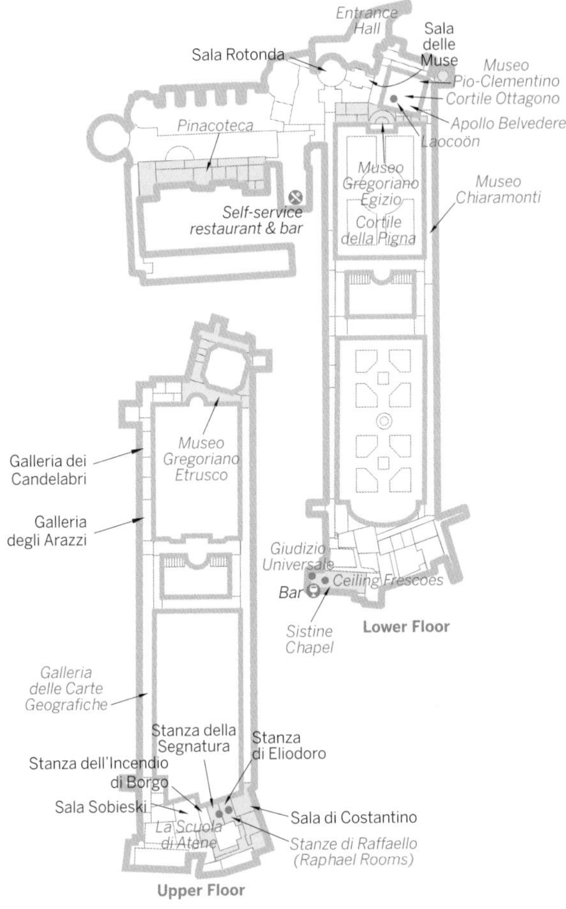
Entrance Hall
Sala delle Muse
Sala Rotonda
Museo Pio-Clementino
Cortile Ottagono
Apollo Belvedere
Laocoön
Pinacoteca
Museo Gregoriano Egizio
Museo Chiaramonti
Self-service restaurant & bar
Cortile della Pigna
Museo Gregoriano Etrusco
Galleria dei Candelabri
Galleria degli Arazzi
Giudizio Universale
Ceiling Frescoes
Bar
Sistine Chapel
Lower Floor
Galleria delle Carte Geografiche
Stanza della Segnatura
Stanza di Eliodoro
Stanza dell'Incendio di Borgo
Sala Sobieski
Sala di Costantino
La Scuola di Atene
Stanze di Raffaello (Raphael Rooms)
Upper Floor

Top Experience

Marvel at St Peter's Basilica

In a city of outstanding churches, none can hold a candle to St Peter's, Italy's largest, richest and most spectacular basilica. A monument to centuries of artistic genius, it boasts many spectacular works of art, including three of Italy's most celebrated masterpieces: Michelangelo's Pietà, his soaring dome, and Bernini's 29m-high baldachin over the papal altar.

MAP P86, C5

Basilica di San Pietro

www.vatican.va

St Peter's Sq

admission free

7am-7pm Apr-Sep, to 6pm Oct-Mar

M Ottaviano-San Pietro

The Facade

Built between 1608 and 1612, Maderno's immense facade is 48m high and 115m wide. Eight 27m-high columns support the upper attic on which 13 statues stand representing Christ the Redeemer, St John the Baptist and the 11 apostles. The central balcony is known as the **Loggia della Benedizione**, and it's from here that the pope delivers his *Urbi et Orbi* blessing at Christmas and Easter.

In the grand atrium, the **Porta Santa** (Holy Door) is opened only in Jubilee years.

Interior – the Nave

Dominating the centre of the basilica is Bernini's 29m-high **baldachin**. Supported by four spiral columns and made with bronze taken from the Pantheon, it stands over the **papal altar**, also known as the Altar of the Confession. In front, Carlo Maderno's **Confessione** stands over the site where St Peter was originally buried.

Above the baldachin, Michelangelo's **dome** soars to a height of 119m. Based on Brunelleschi's design for the Duomo in Florence, it's supported by four massive stone **piers**, each named after the saint whose statue adorns its Bernini-designed niche. The saints are all associated with the basilica's four major relics: the lance **St Longinus** used to pierce Christ's side; the cloth with which **St Veronica** wiped Jesus' face; a fragment of the Cross collected by **St Helena**; and the head of **St Andrew**.

At the base of the **Pier of St Longinus** is Arnolfo di Cambio's much-loved 13th-century bronze **statue of St Peter**, whose right foot has been worn down by centuries of caresses.

Behind the altar, the tribune is home to Bernini's extraordinary **Cattedra di San Pietro**. A vast gilded bronze throne held aloft by four 5m-high saints, it's centred on a wooden seat that was once thought to have been

★ Top Tips

- Dress appropriately if you want to get in – no shorts, miniskirts or bare shoulders.
- Free, two-hour English-language tours are run by seminarians from the Pontifical North American College (www.pnac.org). These generally start at 2.15pm Monday, Wednesday and Friday, leaving from the Ufficio Pellegrini e Turisti (p183). No tickets necessary, but check the website for dates.
- Queues are inevitable at the security checks, but they move quickly.
- Lines are generally shorter during lunch hours and late afternoon.

Take a Break

Head to nearby Prati where you'll find a wide choice of eateries. For a salad or *panino* stop off at organic takeaway Fa-Bìo (p89), while for something more substantial, join the fashionable diners at Il Sorpasso (p90).

NI CAELORVM ✠ TV ES PETRVS
A FIDES
MVNDO

History of the Basilica

The original St Peter's – which lies beneath the current basilica – was commissioned by the Emperor Constantine and built around 349 on the site where St Peter is said to have been buried between AD 64 and 67. But like many medieval churches, it eventually fell into disrepair and it wasn't until the mid-15th century that efforts were made to restore it, first by Pope Nicholas V and then, rather more successfully, by Julius II.

In 1506 construction began on Bramante's design for a new basilica based on a Greek-cross plan. But on Bramante's death in 1514, building ground to a halt as architects, including Raphael and Antonio da Sangallo, tried to modify his original plans. Little progress was made and it wasn't until Michelangelo took over in 1547 at the age of 72 that the situation changed. Michelangelo simplified Bramante's plans and drew up designs for what was to become his greatest architectural achievement, the dome. He never lived to see the cupola built, though, and it was left to Giacomo della Porta and Domenico Fontana to finish it in 1590.

With the dome in place, Carlo Maderno inherited the project in 1605. He designed the monumental facade and lengthened the nave towards the piazza.

The basilica was finally consecrated in 1626.

St Peter's but in fact dates to the 9th century. Above, light shines through a yellow window framed by a gilded mass of golden angels and adorned with a dove to represent the Holy Spirit.

To the right of the throne, Bernini's **monument to Urban VIII** depicts the pope flanked by the figures of Charity and Justice.

Interior – Left Aisle

In the roped-off left transept, the **Cappella della Madonna della Colonna** takes its name from the Madonna that stares out from Giacomo della Porta's marble altar. To its right, above the **tomb of St Leo the Great**, is a fine relief by Alessandro Algardi. Under the next arch is Bernini's last work in the basilica, the **monument to Alexander VII**.

Halfway down the left aisle, the **Cappella Clementina** is named after Clement VIII, who had Giacomo della Porta decorate it for the Jubilee of 1600. Beneath the altar is the **tomb of St Gregory the Great** and, to the left, a **monument to Pope Pius VII** by Thorvaldsen.

The next arch shelters Alessandro Algardi's 16th-century **monument to Leo XI**. Beyond it, the richly decorated **Cappella del Coro** was created by Giovanni Battista Ricci to designs by Giacomo della Porta. The **monument to Innocent VIII** by Antonio

Pollaiuolo in the next aisle arch is a re-creation of a monument from the old basilica.

Continuing on, the **Cappella della Presentazione** contains two of St Peter's most modern works: a black relief **monument to John XXIII** by Emilio Greco, and a **monument to Benedict XV** by Pietro Canonica.

Under the next arch are the so-called **Stuart monuments**. On the right is the monument to Clementina Sobieska, wife of James Stuart, by Filippo Barigioni, and on the left is Canova's vaguely erotic monument to the last three members of the Stuart clan, the pretenders to the English throne who died in exile in Rome.

Interior – Right Aisle

At the head of the right aisle is Michelangelo's hauntingly beautiful **Pietà**. Sculpted when he was only 25 (in 1499), it's the only work the artist ever signed – his signature is etched into the sash across the Madonna's breast.

Nearby, a **red floor disc** marks the spot where Charlemagne and later Holy Roman emperors were crowned by the pope.

On a pillar just beyond the *Pietà*, Carlo Fontana's gilt and bronze **monument to Queen Christina of Sweden** commemorates the far-from-holy Swedish monarch who converted to Catholicism in 1655.

Moving on, you'll come to the **Cappella di San Sebastiano**, home

St Peter's Basilica

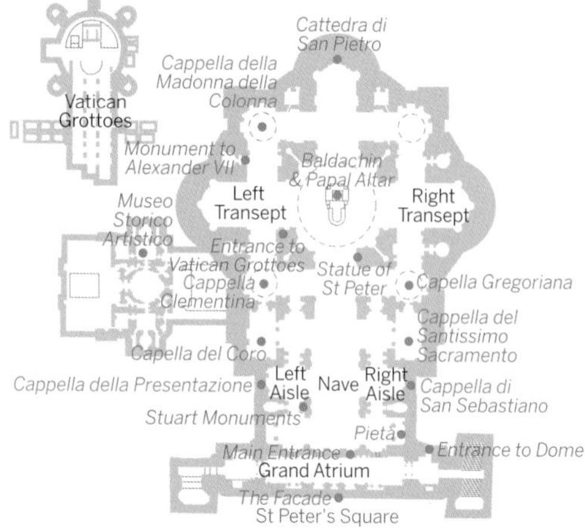

of Pope John Paul II's tomb, and the **Cappella del Santissimo Sacramento**, a sumptuously decorated baroque chapel with works by Borromini, Bernini and Pietro da Cortona.

Beyond the chapel, the grandiose **monument to Gregory XIII** sits near the roped-off **Cappella Gregoriana**, a chapel built by Gregory XIII from designs by Michelangelo.

Much of the right transept is closed off, but you can still make out the **monument to Clement XIII**, one of Canova's most famous works.

Dome

From the entrance to the **dome** (with/without lift €10/8; 8am-6pm Apr-Sep, to 5pm Oct-Mar), on the right of the basilica's main portico, you can walk the 551 steps to the top or take a small lift halfway and then follow on foot for the last 320 steps. Either way, it's a long, steep climb. But make it to the top, and you're rewarded with stunning views from a perch 120m above St Peter's Square.

Museo Storico Artistico

Accessed from the left nave, the **Museo Storico Artistico** (Tesoro, Treasury; 06 6988 1840; €5 incl audioguide; 9am-6.10pm Apr-Sep, to 5.10pm Oct-Mar, last entrance 30min before closing) sparkles with sacred relics. Highlights include a tabernacle by Donatello; the *Colonna Santa*, a 4th-century Byzantine column from the earlier church; and the 6th-century *Crux Vaticana* (Vatican Cross), a jewel-encrusted crucifix presented by the emperor Justinian II to the original basilica.

Vatican Grottoes

Extending beneath the basilica, the **Vatican Grottoes** (admission free; 8am-5pm Apr-Sep, to 4pm Oct-Mar) contain the tombs and sarcophagi of numerous popes, as well as several columns from the original 4th-century basilica. The entrance is in the Pier of St Andrew.

Tomb of St Peter

Excavations beneath the basilica have uncovered part of the original church and what archaeologists believe is the **Tomb of St Peter** (06 6988 5318; www.scavi.va; €13). In 1942 the bones of an elderly, strongly built man were found in a box hidden behind a wall covered by pilgrims' graffiti. And while the Vatican has never definitively claimed that the bones belong to St Peter, in 1968 Pope Paul VI said that they had been identified in a way that the Vatican considered 'convincing'.

The excavations can only be visited by guided tour. For further details, and to book a tour (this must be done well in advance), check out the website of the **Ufficio Scavi** (Excavations Office; Fabbrica di San Pietro; 06 6988 5318; www.scavi.va; €13; 9am-6pm Mon-Fri, to 5pm Sat).

A B C D

1 2 3 4 5 6

For reviews see

Via Faá di Bruno
Via Grazioli Lante
Via S Pellico
Via Barletta
Via della Giuliana
Via Morin
Via Trionfale
Via Bettolo
Largo Trionfale
Via Andrea Doria
Via Otranto
Ottaviano-San Pietro
Via Ostia
12
Via Tunisi
Via Leone IV
Via Candia
Via Silla
10
Via Cipro
Via Candia
Via Vespasiano
Via Ottaviano
Via Germanico
Cipro-Musei Vaticani
Entrance to Vatican Museums
Viale Vaticano
5
Via della Meloria
6
11
Piazza del Risorgimento
Via Angelo Emo
Viale della Zitella
Vatican Museums
14
Vatican Gardens
2
Via della Posta
Via S Porcari
Borgo Angelico
Via di Porta Angelica
Via del Mascherino
VATICAN CITY (CITTÀ DEL VATICANO)
Via del Belvedere
Piazza della Città Leonina
Via dei Corridori
St Peter's Basilica
St Peter's Square
3
Piazza Pio XII
Piazza Santa Marta
Piazza dei P Romani
Ufficio Pellegrini e Turisti
Via Paolo VI
Piazza di Sant'Uffizio
Via Aurelia
Via di Porta Cavalleggeri
Via del Crocefisso

A B C D

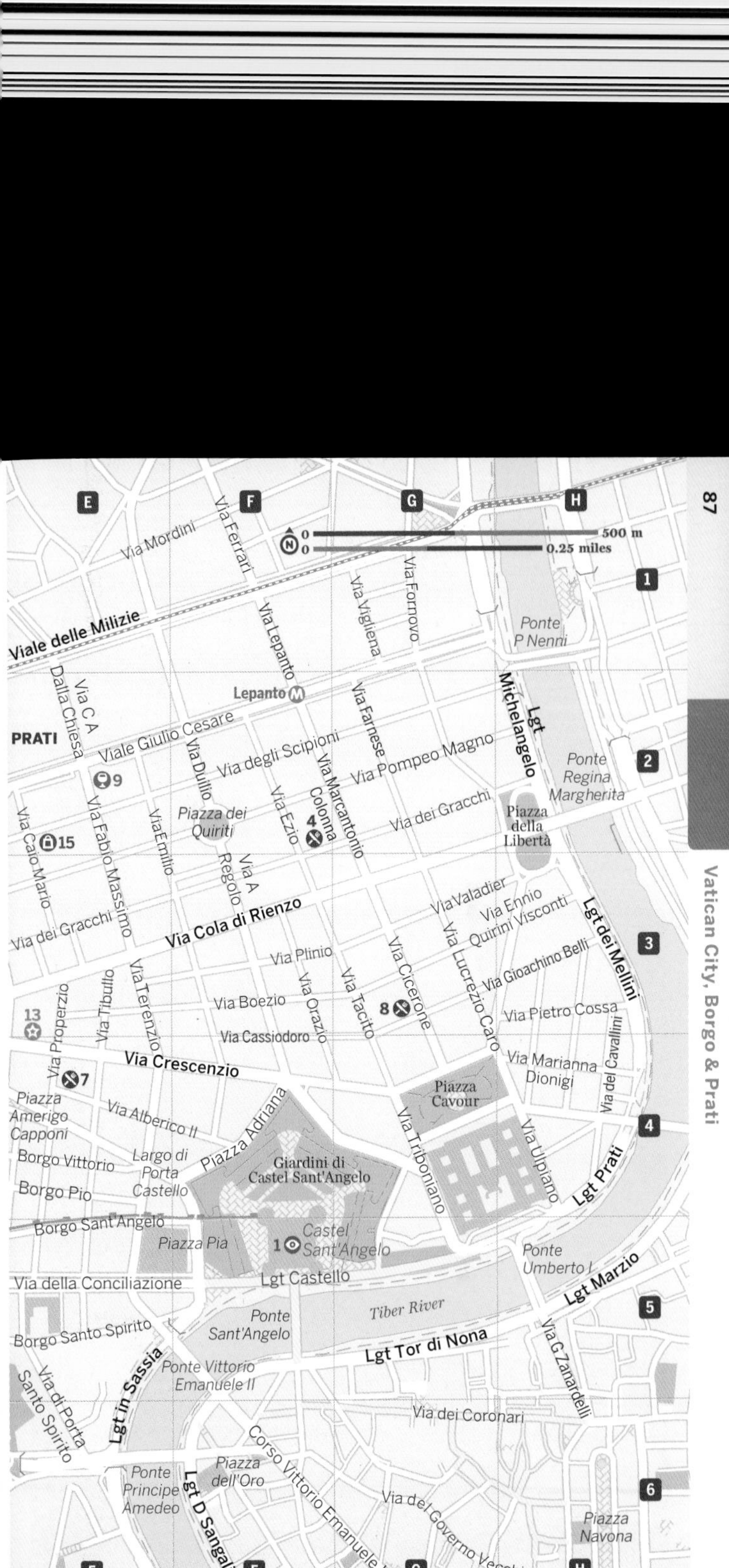
E
F
G
H
1
2
3
4
5
6
0
500 m
0.25 miles
Via Mordini
Via Ferrari
Viale delle Milizie
Via Lepanto
Via Vigliena
Via Fornovo
Ponte P Nenni
Lepanto
Lgt Michelangelo
PRATI
Via C A Dalla Chiesa
Viale Giulio Cesare
Via Dullio
Via degli Scipioni
Via Farnese
Via Marcantonio Colonna
Via Pompeo Magno
Ponte Regina Margherita
9
Via Caio Mario
15
Via Fabio Massimo
ViaEmilio
Piazza dei Quiriti
Via Ezio
4
Via dei Gracchi
Piazza della Libertà
Via A Regolo
Via Valadier
Via Ennio Quirini Visconti
Lgt dei Mellini
Via dei Gracchi
Via Cola di Rienzo
Via Plinio
Via Lucrezio Caro
Via Gioachino Belli
Via Cicerone
Via Tibullo
Via Terenzio
Via Boezio
Via Orazio
Via Tacito
8
Via Pietro Cossa
13
Via Properzio
Via Cassiodoro
Via Crescenzio
Via Marianna Dionigi
Via del Cavallini
7
Piazza Amerigo Capponi
Via Alberico II
Piazza Adriana
Piazza Cavour
Via Triboniano
Via Ulpiano
Borgo Vittorio
Largo di Porta Castello
Giardini di Castel Sant'Angelo
Lgt Prati
Borgo Pio
Borgo Sant'Angelo
Piazza Pia
Castel Sant'Angelo
1
Ponte Umberto I
Via della Conciliazione
Lgt Castello
Lgt Marzio
Ponte Sant'Angelo
Tiber River
Borgo Santo Spirito
Lgt Tor di Nona
Via G Zanardelli
Lgt in Sassia
Ponte Vittorio Emanuele II
Via di Porta Santo Spirito
Via dei Coronari
Corso Vittorio Emanuele II
Piazza dell'Oro
Ponte Principe Amedeo
Lgt D Sangallo
Via del Governo Vecchio
Piazza Navona

Sights

Castel Sant'Angelo

MUSEUM, CASTLE

1 MAP P86, F5

With its chunky round keep, this castle is an instantly recognisable landmark. Built as a mausoleum for the emperor Hadrian, it was converted into a papal fortress in the 6th century and named after an angelic vision that Pope Gregory the Great had in 590. Nowadays it is a moody and dramatic keep that houses the **Museo Nazionale di Castel Sant'Angelo** and its grand collection of paintings, sculpture, military memorabilia and medieval firearms. (06 681 91 11; www.castelsantangelo.beniculturali.it; Lungotevere Castello 50; adult/reduced €14/7, free 1st Sunday of the month Oct-Mar; 9am-7.30pm, ticket office to 6.30pm; Piazza Pia)

Vatican Gardens

GARDENS

2 MAP P86, B4

Up to a third of the Vatican is covered by the perfectly manicured Vatican Gardens, which contain fortifications, grottoes, monuments, fountains, and the state's tiny heliport and train station. Visits are by guided tour only – either on foot (two hours) or by open-air bus (45 minutes) – for which you'll need to book at least a week in advance. After the tour you're free to visit the Vatican Museums on your own; admission is included in the ticket price. (www.museivaticani.va; adult/reduced incl Vatican Museums

Castel Sant'Angelo

€33/24, by open-air bus €37/23; by reservation only; Piazza del Risorgimento, M Ottaviano-San Pietro)

St Peter's Square

PIAZZA

3 MAP P86, D5

Overlooked by St Peter's Basilica (p80), the Vatican's central square was laid out between 1656 and 1667 to a design by Gian Lorenzo Bernini. Seen from above, it resembles a giant keyhole with two semicircular colonnades, each consisting of four rows of Doric columns, encircling a giant ellipse that straightens out to funnel believers into the basilica. The effect was deliberate – Bernini described the colonnades as representing 'the motherly arms of the church'. (Piazza San Pietro; Piazza del Risorgimento, M Ottaviano-San Pietro)

Papal Audiences

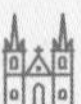

Papal audiences are held at 10am on Wednesdays, usually in St Peter's Square but sometimes in the nearby Aula delle Udienze Pontificie Paolo VI (Paul VI Audience Hall). You'll need to book free tickets in advance. No tickets are required for the pope's Sunday blessing, at noon in St Peter's Square. See the Vatican website (www.vatican.va) for more details.

Eating

Gelateria dei Gracchi

GELATO €

4 MAP P86, F2

The original location of the small chain of gelato shops that has taken Rome by storm. The proprietors here only use fresh fruit in season — no fruit concentrate, no peach gelato in January etc. The flavours vary by day and season, but you're always assured of a top treat. Try one of the chocolate-covered gelato bars. (06 321 66 68; www.gelateriadeigracchi.it; Via dei Gracchi 272; gelato from €2.50; noon-12.30am; Piazza Cola Di Rienzo)

Fa-Bìo

SANDWICHES €

5 MAP P86, D3

Sandwiches, wraps, salads and fresh juices are all prepared with speed, skill and fresh organic ingredients at this busy takeaway. Locals, Vatican tour guides and in-the-know visitors come here to grab a quick lunchtime bite. If you can't find room in the small interior, there are stools along the pavement. (06 3974 6510; Via Germanico 71; meals €5-7; 10.30am-5.30pm Mon-Fri, to 4pm Sat; Piazza del Risorgimento, M Ottaviano-San Pietro)

Bonci Pizzarium

PIZZA €

6 MAP P86, A3

Pizzarium, the takeaway of Gabriele Bonci, Rome's acclaimed pizza emperor, serves Rome's best sliced pizza, bar none. Scissor-cut squares of soft, springy base are topped with original combinations of seasonal ingredients and served for immediate consumption. It's often jammed: there are only a couple of benches and stools for the tourist hordes; head across to the plaza at the metro station for a seat. (☎06 3974 5416; www.bonci.it; Via della Meloria 43; pizza slices €5; ⏰11am-10pm Mon-Sat, from noon Sun; Ⓜ Cipro)

Il Sorpasso ITALIAN €€

7 MAP P86, E4

A bar-restaurant hybrid sporting a vintage cool look – vaulted stone ceilings, exposed brick, rustic wooden tables, summertime outdoor seating – Il Sorpasso is a Prati hot spot. Open throughout the day, it caters to a fashionable crowd, serving everything from salads and pasta specials to *trapizzini* (pyramids of stuffed pizza), cured meats and cocktails. (☎06 8902 4554; www.sorpasso.info; Via Properzio 31-33; meals €20-35; ⏰7.30am-1am Mon-Fri, 9am-1am Sat; 📶; 🚌Piazza del Risorgimento)

L'Arcangelo LAZIO €€€

8 MAP P86, G3

Styled as a bistro with wood panelling, leather banquettes and casual table settings, L'Arcangelo enjoys a stellar local reputation. Dishes are modern and creative yet still undeniably Roman in their use of traditional ingredients such as sweetbreads and *baccalà* (cod). A further plus is the well-curated wine list. (☎06 321 09 92; www.larcangelo.com; Via Giuseppe Gioachino Belli 59; meals €45-80, lunch set menu €30; ⏰1-2.30pm Mon-Fri, 8-11pm Mon-Sat; 🚌Piazza Cavour)

Drinking

Sciascia Caffè CAFE

9 MAP P86, E2

There are several contenders for the best coffee in town, but in our opinion nothing tops the *caffè eccellente* served at this polished old-school cafe. A velvety smooth espresso served in a delicate cup lined with melted chocolate, it's nothing short of magnificent, and has been since 1919. (☎06 321 15 80; http://sciasciacaffe1919.it; Via Fabio Massimo 80/a; ⏰7am-9pm; Ⓜ Ottaviano-San Pietro)

L'Osteria di Birra del Borgo Roma CRAFT BEER

10 MAP P86, D3

Italy is no longer just about wine; for years a generation of brewers has been developing great craft beers. Try some of the best at this chic, contemporary bar with a soaring ceiling and stylish vats of brewing beer. It has a short menu of Italian standards at night and fine antipasto choices all day. (☎06 8376 2316; http://osteria.birradelborgo.it; Via Silla 26; ⏰noon-2am; Ⓜ Ottaviano-San Pietro)

Be.Re. CRAFT BEER

11 MAP P86, C3

With its exposed-brick decor, high vaulted ceilings and narrow pavement tables, this is a good spot for Italian craft beers. And should hunger strike, there's a branch of hit takeaway Trapizzino right next door that offers table service at Be.Re. Picky coffee drinkers will enjoy the attached Pergamino as it includes concoctions made with soy milk. (06 9442 1854; www.be-re.eu; Piazza del Risorgimento, cnr Via Vespasiano; 11am-2am; Piazza del Risorgimento)

Entertainment

Alexanderplatz JAZZ

12 MAP P86, C2

Intimate, underground and hard to find – look for the discreet black door near the corner – Rome's most celebrated jazz club draws top Italian and international performers and a respectful cosmopolitan crowd. Book a table for the best stage views or to dine here, although note that it's the music that's the star act. Performances begin at 10pm. (06 8377 5604; www.alexanderplatzjazzclub.com; Via Ostia 9; tickets €15-20; 8.30pm-1.30am; M Ottaviano-San Pietro)

Fonclea LIVE MUSIC

13 MAP P86, E3

Fonclea is a great little pub venue, with nightly gigs by bands playing everything from jazz and soul to pop, rock and doo-wop. Get in the mood with a drink during happy hour (6pm to 8.30pm daily). There are several cocktail bars nearby with outdoor tables. (06 689 63 02; www.fonclea.it; Via Crescenzio 82a; cover after 8pm €10; 6pm-2am Sep-May, concerts 9.30pm; ; Piazza del Risorgimento)

Shopping

Paciotti Salumeria FOOD & DRINKS

14 MAP P86, A4

This family-run deli is a fantasyland of Italian edibles. Whole Prosciutto hams hang in profusion. Cheeses, olive oil, dried pasta, balsamic vinegar, wine and truffle pâtés crowd the shelves, and can be bubble-wrapped and vacuum-sealed for travel. Patriarch Antonio Paciotti and his three affable sons merrily advise customers in both Italian and English. (06 3973 3646; www.paciottisalumeria.it; Via Marcantonio Bragadin 51/53; 7.30am-8.30pm Mon-Wed, Fri & Sat, 12.30-8.30pm Thu; M Cipro)

Il Sellaio FASHION & ACCESSORIES

15 MAP P86, E2

During the 1960s Ferruccio Serafini was one of Rome's most sought-after artisans, making handmade leather shoes and bags for the likes of Liz Taylor and Marlon Brando. Nowadays his daughter Francesca runs the family shop where you can pick up beautiful hand-stitched bags, belts and accessories. Have designs made to order or get your leather handbags and luggage reconditioned. (06 321 17 19; www.serafinipelletteria.it; Via Caio Mario 14; 9.30am-7.30pm Mon-Fri, 9.30am-1pm & 3.30-7.30pm Sat; M Ottaviano-San Pietro)

Tridente, Trevi & the Quirinale

Counting the Trevi Fountain and Spanish Steps among its A-list sights, this part of Rome is debonair and touristy. Designer boutiques, fashionable bars and historic cafes crowd the streets of Tridente, while the area around Piazza Barberini and the Trevi Fountain, within shouting distance of the presidential Quirinale palace, harbours multiple art galleries and eateries.

The Short List

- ***Spanish Steps (p96)*** *People-watching and selfie-snapping while climbing this city icon.*
- **Basilica di Santa Maria del Popolo (p102)** *Marvelling at Caravaggio's two masterworks in the Cerasi Chapel.*
- **Villa Medici (p101)** *Touring this Renaissance villa with its formal gardens and wonderful city views.*
- **Gallerie Nazionali: Palazzo Barberini (p100)** *Admiring works by Raphael, Caravaggio, El Greco and Pietro da Cortona in a palace built for a pope.*
- ***Shopping streets (p110)*** *Browsing designer fashions, artisanal perfumes, silverware, and much more besides, on and around Via dei Condotti.*

Getting There & Around

M Barberini for the Trevi and Quirinale areas; Spagna and Flaminio for Tridente. All three stations are on line A.

Numerous buses serve Piazza Barberini; many stop at the southern end of Via del Corso and on Via del Tritone for Tridente.

Tridente, Trevi & the Quirinale Map on p98

Chiesa di Santa Maria della Vittoria (p103) STEFANO_VALERI / SHUTTERSTOCK ©

Top Experience 

Throw a coin in the Trevi Fountain

Rome's most famous fountain, the iconic Fontana di Trevi, is a baroque extravaganza – a foaming white-marble and emerald-water masterpiece filling an entire piazza. The flamboyant ensemble, 20m wide and 26m high, was designed by Nicola Salvi in 1732 and depicts the chariot of the sea-god Oceanus being led by Tritons accompanying seahorses that represent the moods of the sea.

MAP P98, D6

Fontana di Trevi

Piazza di Trevi

M Barberini

Aqua Virgo

The fountain's water comes from the Aqua Virgo, an underground aqueduct that is over 2000 years old. It was built by General Agrippa under Augustus and brings water from the Salone springs around 19km away. The *tre vie* (three roads) that converge at the fountain give it its name.

Salvi's Urn

To the eastern side of the fountain is a large round stone urn. The story goes that during the fountain's construction, Salvi was harassed by a barber, who had a nearby shop and was critical of the work in progress. Thus the sculptor added this urn in order to block the irritating critic.

Coin Tossing

The famous tradition (inaugurated in the 1954 film *Three Coins in the Fountain*) is to toss a coin into the fountain, thus ensuring your return to Rome. An estimated €3000 is thrown into the Trevi each day. This money is collected daily and goes to the Catholic charity Caritas, with its yield increasing significantly since the crackdown on people extracting the money for themselves.

Trevi on Camera

Most famously, Trevi Fountain is where movie star Anita Ekberg cavorted in Federico Fellini's classic *La Dolce Vita* (1960); apparently she wore waders under her iconic black dress but still shivered during the winter shoot.

In 2016 fashion house Fendi staged a show at the fountain following its €2.18 million sponsorship of the fountain's restoration.

★ Top Tips

- Coin-tossing etiquette: throw with your right hand, over your left shoulder with your back facing the fountain.
- Paddling or bathing in the fountain is strictly forbidden, as is eating and drinking on the steps leading down to the water. Both crimes risk an on-the-spot fine of up to €500.
- The fountain gets very busy during the day; visit later in the evening when it's beautifully lit instead.

✗ Take a Break

Recommended dining choices near the fountain include Il Chianti (p106), specialising in hearty Tuscan fare, and Hostaria Romana (p105), a model Roman trattoria.

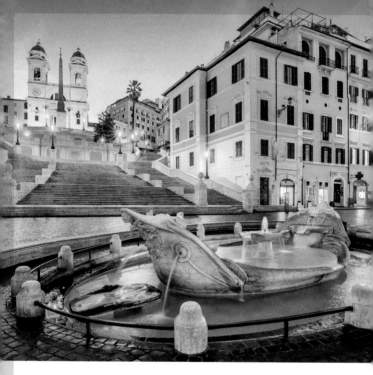

Top Experience 

Climb the Spanish Steps & explore Piazza di Spagna

Forming a picture-perfect backdrop to Piazza di Spagna, this statement sweep of stairs is one of the city's major icons and public meeting points. Though officially named the Scalinata della Trinità dei Monti, the stairs are popularly called the Spanish Steps.

MAP P98, C4

M Spagna

Spanish Steps

Piazza di Spagna was named after the Spanish Embassy to the Holy See, but the staircase – 135 gleaming steps designed by the Italian Francesco de Sanctis – was built in 1725 with a legacy from the French. The dazzling stairs reopened in September 2016 after a €1.5 million clean-up job funded by Bulgari jewellers.

Chiesa della Trinità dei Monti

This landmark **church** (Map p98, D3; http://trinitadeimonti.net/it/chiesa; 10.15am-8pm Tue-Thu, noon-9pm Fri, 9.15am-8pm Sat, 9am-8pm Sun) was commissioned by Louis XII of France and consecrated in 1585. It's notable for its great city views and frescoes by Daniele da Volterra.

Keats-Shelley House

Overlooking the Steps, this **house-museum** (www.keats-shelley-house.org; adult/reduced €5/4; 10am-1pm & 2-6pm Mon-Sat) is where Romantic poet John Keats died in February 1821. Keats came to Rome in 1820 to try to improve his health, and rented two rooms with a painter companion, Joseph Severn (1793–1879).

Fontana della Barcaccia

At the foot of the steps, the fountain of a sinking boat, the **Barcaccia** (1627), is believed to be by Pietro Bernini, father of the more famous Gian Lorenzo. The sunken design is a clever piece of engineering to compensate for low water pressure – it's fed by an ancient Roman aqueduct, the Aqua Virgo.

Colonna dell'Immacolata

To the southeast of the piazza, adjacent Piazza Mignanelli is dominated by the Colonna dell'Immacolata, built in 1857 to celebrate Pope Pius IX's declaration of the Immaculate Conception.

★ Top Tips

- No picnics on the steps, please! It is forbidden to eat and drink or 'shout, squall and sing' on the beautifully restored staircase. Doing so risks a fine of up to €500.
- A prime photo op is during the springtime festival Mostra delle Azalee, held late March/early April, when hundreds of vases of bright pink azaleas in bloom adorn the steps.
- To skip the 135-step hike up, take the lift inside the Spagna metro station to the top.

Take a Break

Play the Grand Tour tourist with morning or afternoon tea at 19th-century Babington's Tea Rooms (p106), at the foot of the Spanish Steps.

Watch the sun set over the steps from the fabulous ringside terrace of cocktail bar Il Palazzetto (p107).

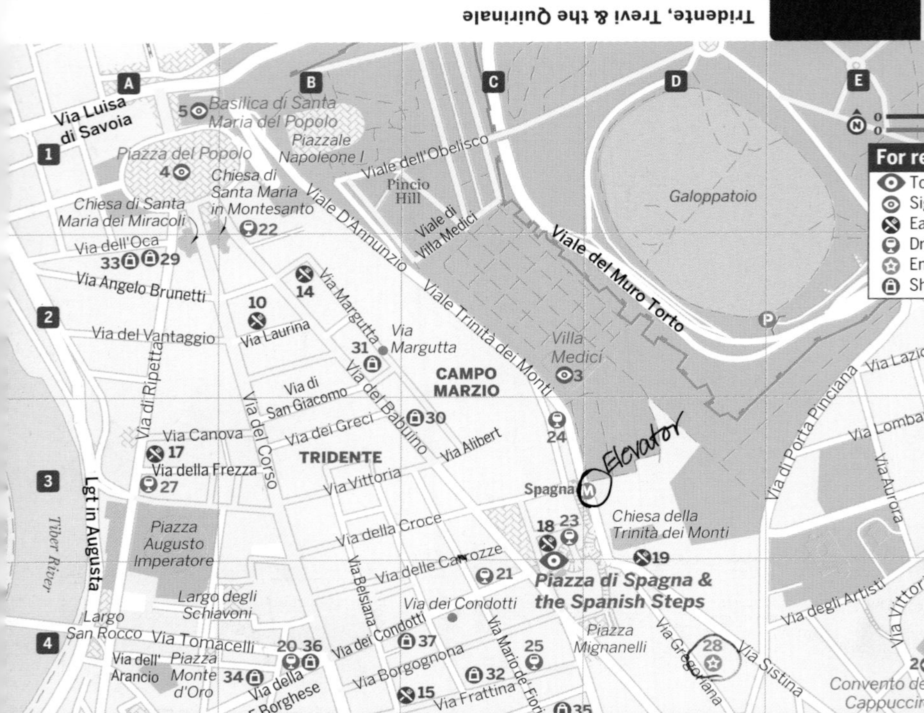
For reviews see
Top Experiences p94
Sights p100
Eating p104
Drinking p106
Entertainment p108
Shopping p109
0 200 m
0 0.1 miles
A
B
C
D
E
F
1
2
3
4
Via Luisa di Savoia
Basilica di Santa Maria del Popolo
Piazzale Napoleone I
Piazza del Popolo
Chiesa di Santa Maria in Montesanto
Chiesa di Santa Maria dei Miracoli
Via dell'Oca
Via Angelo Brunetti
Via del Vantaggio
Via di Ripetta
Via Canova
Via della Frezza
Lgt in Augusta
Tiber River
Piazza Augusto Imperatore
Largo degli Schiavoni
Largo San Rocco
Via Tomacelli
Via dell' Arancio
Piazza Monte d'Oro
Via della F Borghese
Via Laurina
Via Margutta
Via di San Giacomo
Via del Corso
Via dei Greci
TRIDENTE
Via Vittoria
Via del Babuino
CAMPO MARZIO
Via Alibert
Via della Croce
Via Belsiana
Via delle Carrozze
Via dei Condotti
Via Borgognona
Via Frattina
Via Mario de' Fiori
Viale dell'Obelisco
Pincio Hill
Viale D'Annunzio
Viale di Villa Medici
Viale Trinità dei Monti
Villa Medici
Viale del Muro Torto
Galoppatoio
Spagna
Elevator
Chiesa della Trinità dei Monti
Piazza di Spagna & the Spanish Steps
Piazza Mignanelli
Via Gregoriana
Via Sistina
Via di Porta Pinciana
Via Lazio
Via Lombardia
Via Aurora
Via Emilia
Via Vittorio Veneto
Via Liguria
Via degli Artisti
Via Sardegna
Via Marche
Convento dei Cappuccini
Via di San Basilio
Via di San Nicola da Tolentino
Via Barberini
5
4
22
33
29
10
14
31
30
3
24
17
27
18
23
19
21
20
36
34
37
25
32
15
35
28
2

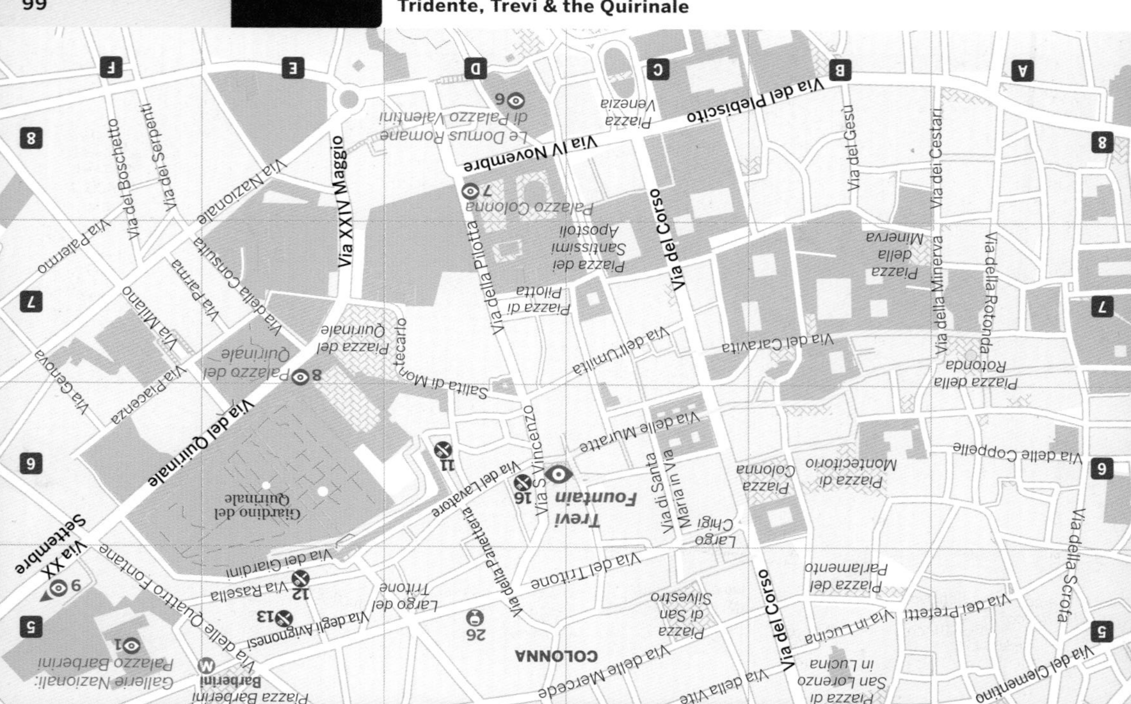
Via XX Settembre
9
5
Gallerie Nazionali: Palazzo Barberini
1
Via delle Quattro Fontane
Piazza Barberini
Barberini
Via del Quirinale
Giardino del Quirinale
Via Genova
Via Piacenza
Via Milano
Via Palermo
Via del Boschetto
Via dei Serpenti
Via Parma
Via della Consulta
Via Nazionale
Palazzo del Quirinale
8
Piazza del Quirinale
Via XXIV Maggio
Via degli Avignonesi
13
12
Via Rasella
Via dei Giardini
Largo del Tritone
Salita di Montecarlo
11
26
Via della Panetteria
Via del Lavatore
COLONNA
16
Via S Vincenzo
Via della Pilotta
Palazzo Colonna
7
Le Domus Romane di Palazzo Valentini
6
Trevi Fountain
Via del Tritone
Via delle Mercede
Piazza di Pilotta
Piazza dei Santissimi Apostoli
Via IV Novembre
Piazza Venezia
Via di Santa Maria in Via
Via delle Muratte
Via dell'Umiltà
Piazza di San Silvestro
Largo Chigi
Via del Corso
Via della Vite
Piazza Colonna
Piazza di San Lorenzo in Lucina
Via in Lucina
Piazza del Parlamento
Piazza di Montecitorio
Via del Caravita
Via del Plebiscito
Via del Gesù
Piazza della Minerva
Via della Minerva
Via dei Cestari
Via dei Prefetti
Via delle Coppelle
Piazza della Rotonda
Via della Rotonda
Via del Clementino
Via della Scrofa
A
B
C
D
E
F

Sights

Gallerie Nazionali: Palazzo Barberini GALLERY

1 MAP P98, F5

Commissioned to celebrate the Barberini family's rise to papal power, this sumptuous baroque palace impresses even before you view its breathtaking art collection. Many high-profile architects worked on it, including rivals Bernini and Borromini; the former contributed a square staircase, the latter a helicoidal one. Amid the masterpieces on display, don't miss Filippo Lippi's *Annunciazione* (*Annunciation*; 1440–45) and Pietro da Cortona's ceiling fresco *Il Trionfo della Divina Provvidenza* (*The Triumph of Divine Providence*; 1632–39). (Galleria Nazionale d'Arte Antica; 06 481 45 91; www.barberinicorsini.org; Via delle Quattro Fontane 13; adult/reduced €12/6; 8.30am-6pm Tue-Sun; M Barberini)

Convento dei Cappuccini MUSEUM

2 MAP P98, E4

This church and convent complex safeguards what is possibly Rome's strangest sight: crypt chapels where everything from the picture frames to the light fittings is made of human bones. Between 1732 and 1775 resident Capuchin monks used the bones of 3700 of their departed brothers to create this macabre *memento mori* (reminder of death) – a 30m-long passageway ensnaring six crypts, each

Piazza del Popolo

named after the type of bone used to decorate (skulls, shin bones, pelvises etc). (☎06 8880 3695; www.cappucciniviaveneto.it; Via Vittorio Veneto 27; adult/reduced €8.50/5; ⏲9am-6.30pm; Ⓜ Barberini)

Villa Medici

PALACE

3 MAP P98, C2

Built for Cardinal Ricci da Montepulciano in 1540, this sumptuous Renaissance palace was purchased by Ferdinando de' Medici in 1576 and remained in Medici hands until 1801, when Napoleon acquired it for the French Academy. Guided tours (1½ hours) in multiple languages take in the sculpture-filled gardens and orchard, a garden studio exquisitely frescoed by Jacopo Zucchi in 1577 and the cardinal's private apartments. Note the pieces of ancient Roman sculpture from the Ara Pacis embedded in the villa's walls. (☎06 676 13 11; www.villamedici.it; Viale Trinità dei Monti 1; guided tour adult/reduced €12/6; ⏲10am-7pm Tue-Sun; Ⓜ Spagna)

Piazza del Popolo

PIAZZA

4 MAP P98, A1

This massive piazza was laid out in 1538 to provide a grandiose entrance to what was then Rome's main northern gateway. It has since been remodelled several times, most recently by Giuseppe Valadier in 1823. Standing sentinel at its southern approach are Carlo Rainaldi's twin 17th-century churches, **Chiesa di Santa Maria dei Miracoli** (Map p98, A1; ☎06 361 02 50; Via del Corso 528; ⏲7.30am-12.30pm & 4.30-7.30pm) and **Basilica di Santa Maria in Montesanto** (Chiesa degli Artisti; Map p98, A1; www.chiesadegliartisti.it; Via del Babuino 198; ⏲10am-noon & 5-8pm Mon-Fri, 10am-noon Sat, 11am-1.30pm Sun). In the centre, the 36m-high **obelisk** was brought by Augustus from ancient Egypt; it originally stood in the Circo Massimo. (Ⓜ Flaminio)

Via Margutta

Small antique shops, commercial art galleries and artisanal boutiques are arrayed along **Via Margutta** (Map p98, B2; Ⓜ Spagna), one of Rome's prettiest pedestrian cobbled lanes. Strung with ivy-laced *palazzi*, the street is named after a 16th-century family of barbers but has long been associated with art and artists: Picasso worked at a gallery at No 54 and the Italian Futurists had their first meeting here in 1917. Audrey Hepburn and Gregory Peck whispered sweet nothings to each other in Joe Badley's apartment at No 51 in the classic movie *Roman Holiday* (1953). Of the street's more recent residents, the most famous is film director Federico Fellini, who lived at No 110 with his wife Giulietta Masina until his death in 1993.

Rome on Film

The Golden Age

For the golden age of Roman film-making you have to turn the clocks back to the 1940s, when Roberto Rossellini (1906–77) produced a trio of neorealist masterpieces. The first and most famous was *Roma città aperta* (Rome Open City; 1945), filmed in the Prenestina district. Vittorio de Sica (1901–74) kept the neorealist ball rolling in 1948 with *Ladri di biciclette* (Bicycle Thieves), again filmed in Rome's sprawling suburbs.

Federico Fellini (1920–94) took the creative baton from the neorealists and carried it into the following decades. His greatest international hit was *La Dolce Vita* (1960), starring Marcello Mastroianni and Anita Ekberg.

Contemporary Directors

Born in Naples but Roman by adoption, Paolo Sorrentino (b 1970) is the big name in Italian cinema right now. Since winning an Oscar for his 2013 hit *La grande bellezza* (The Great Beauty), he has directed Michael Caine and Harvey Keitel in *Youth* (2015) and Jude Law in the HBO–Atlantic Sky series *The Young Pope* (2016) and *The New Pope* (2019).

In contrast to Sorrentino, a Neapolitan best known for a film about Rome, Matteo Garrone (b 1968) is a Roman famous for a film about Naples. *Gomorra* (Gomorrah; 2008), his hard-hitting exposé of the Neapolitan Camorra (Mafia), enjoyed widespread acclaim. His latest work is *Dogman* (2018), filmed around Rome, Lazio and Campania.

On Location in Rome

Villa Borghese and the Terme di Caracalla were among the locations for Ben Stiller's camp fashion romp *Zoolander 2* (2016), while the Tiber riverside and Via della Conciliazione both appeared in the James Bond outing, *Spectre* (2015).

Basilica di Santa Maria del Popolo

BASILICA

5  MAP P98, A1

One of Rome's richest Renaissance churches, with a particularly impressive collection of art, including two Caravaggios: the *Conversion of St Paul* (1600–1601) and the *Crucifixion of St Peter* (1601). These are located in the 16th-century **Cerasi Chapel** to the left of the main altar. Other fine works include Caracci's *Assumption of the Virgin* (c 1660) in the same chapel and multiple frescoes by Pinturicchio –

look for his 1484–90 *Adoration of the Christ Child* in the **Della Rovere Chapel**. (☎392 3612243; www.smariadelpopolo.com; Piazza del Popolo 12; ⏰7am-noon & 4-7pm Mon-Sat, 8am-1.30pm & 4.30-7.30pm Sun; Ⓜ Flaminio)

Le Domus Romane di Palazzo Valentini ARCHAEOLOGICAL SITE

6 MAP P98, D8

Underneath a grand mansion that's been the seat of the Province of Rome since 1873 lie the archaeological remains of several lavish ancient Roman houses; the excavated fragments have been turned into a fascinating multimedia 'experience'. Tours are every 30 minutes, but alternate between Italian, English, French, German and Spanish. Book ahead online or by phone (advance booking fee €1.50), especially during holiday periods. (☎06 2276 1280; www.palazzovalentini.it; Via Foro Traiano 85; adult/reduced €12/8; ⏰9.30am-6.30pm Wed-Mon; 👪; Ⓜ Barberini)

Palazzo Colonna GALLERY

7 MAP P98, D8

The guided tours of this opulent palace are among the city's best, introducing visitors to the residence and art collection of the patrician Colonna family. The largest private palace in Rome, it has a formal garden, multiple reception rooms and a grandiose baroque Great Hall built to honour Marcantonio II Colonna, a hero of the 1571 Battle of Lepanto. Guides recount plenty of anecdotes about family members including fascinating Maria Mancini Mazzarino, a feisty favourite of Louis XIV of France. (☎06 678 43 50; www.galleriacolonna.it; Via della Pilotta 17; adult/reduced €12/10; ⏰9am-1.15pm Sat, closed Aug; Ⓜ Colosseo)

Palazzo del Quirinale PALACE

8 MAP P98, E7

Perched atop the Quirinale Hill, one of Rome's seven hills, this former papal summer residence has been home to the Italian head of state since 1948. Originally commissioned by Pope Gregory XIII (r 1572–85), it was built and added to over 150 years by architects including Ottaviano Mascherino, Domenico Fontana, Francesco Borromini, Gian Lorenzo Bernini and Carlo Maderno. Guided tours of its grand reception rooms should be booked at least five days ahead by telephone, or online at www.coopculture.it. (☎06 3996 75 57; www.quirinale.it; Piazza del Quirinale; tours from €1.50; ⏰9.30am-4pm Tue, Wed & Fri-Sun, closed Aug; 🚌Via Nazionale, Ⓜ Repubblica)

Chiesa di Santa Maria della Vittoria CHURCH

9 MAP P98, F5

Designed by Carlo Maderno, this modest church is an unlikely setting for an extraordinary work of art – Bernini's extravagant and sexually charged *Santa Teresa trafitta dall'amore di Dio* (*Ecstasy of St Teresa*). This daring sculpture depicts Teresa, engulfed in the folds of a flowing cloak, floating in ecstasy on a cloud while a teasing angel pierces her repeatedly with a golden arrow. It's in the fourth chapel on the north side. (06 4274 0571; www.chiesasantamariavittoriaroma.it; Via XX Settembre 17; 7am-noon & 3.30-7.15pm; M Repubblica)

Eating

Fatamorgana Corso GELATO €

10 MAP P98, B2

The wonderful all-natural, gluten-free gelato served at Fatamorgana is arguably Rome's best artisanal ice cream. Innovative and classic ambrosial flavours abound, all made from the finest seasonal ingredients. There are several branches around town. (06 3265 22 38; www.gelateriafatamorgana.com; Via Laurina 10; cups & cones €2.50-5; noon-11pm; M Flaminio)

Piccolo Arancio TRATTORIA €€

11 MAP P98, D6

In a 'hood riddled with tourist traps, this backstreet trattoria – tucked inside a little house next to grandiose Palazzo Scanderberg – stands out. The kitchen mixes Roman classics with more contemporary options and, unusually, includes a hefty number of seafood choices – the *linguini alla pescatora* (handmade pasta with shellfish and baby tomatoes) is sensational. Bookings essential. (06 678 61 39; www.piccoloarancio.it; Vicolo Scanderbeg 112; meals €38;

Il Margutta

ALEXANDRA BRUZZESE / LONELY PLANET ©

noon-3pm & 7pm-midnight Tue-Sun; M Barberini)

Hostaria Romana

TRATTORIA €€

12 MAP P98, E5

Beloved of locals and tourists alike, this bustling place in Trevi is everything an Italian trattoria should be. Order an antipasto or pasta (excellent) and then move onto a main – traditional Roman dishes including *saltimbocca* and tripe are on offer, as are lots of grilled meats. If you'relucky, your meal may be rounded off with complimentary *biscotti*. Bookings highly recommended. (06 474 52 84; www.hostariaromana.it; Via del Boccaccio 1; meals €45; 12.30-3pm & 7.15-11pm Mon-Sat; M Barberini)

Colline Emiliane

ITALIAN €€

13 MAP P98, E5

Serving incredible regional cuisine from Emilia-Romagna, this restaurant has been operated by the Latini family since 1931; the current owners are Paola (dessert queen) and Anna (watch her making pasta each morning in the glassed-off lab). Our three recommendations when eating here: start with the *antipasti della casa* (€26 for two people), progress to pasta and don't scrimp on dessert. (06 481 75 38; www.collineemiliane.com; Via degli Avignonesi 22; meals €45; 12.45-2.45pm & 7.30-10.45pm Tue-Sat, 12.45-2.45pm Sun; M Barberini)

Il Margutta

VEGETARIAN €€

14 MAP P98, B2

This chic gallery-bar-restaurant is packed at lunchtime with Romans feasting on its good-value, eat-as-much-as-you-can buffet deal. Everything on its menu is organic, and the evening menu is particularly creative – vegetables and pulses combined and presented with care and flair. Among the various tasting menus available is a vegan option. (06 3265 0577; www.ilmargutta.bio; Via Margutta 118; lunch buffet weekdays/weekends €15/25, meals €35; 8.30am-11.30pm; ; M Spagna)

VyTA Enoteca Regionale del Lazio

LAZIO €€

15 MAP P98, C4

Showcasing food and wine of the Lazio region, this mega-stylish address owes its design to fashionable Roman architect Daniela Colli and its contemporary menu to chef Dino De Bellis. The burnished copper bar is a perfect perch for enjoying *panini*, *cicheti* (snacks) and *taglieri* (cheese and meat plates) – it also offers a tempting *aperitivo* spread. Upstairs, a glam restaurant awaits. (06 8771 60 18; www.vytaenotecalazio.it/en; Via Frattina 94; cicchetti from €3, platters €15, restaurant meals €55; 9am-11pm Sun-Thu, to midnight Fri & Sat; M Spagna)

Il Chianti

TUSCAN €€

16 MAP P98, D6

The name says it all: this pretty ivy-clad place specialises in Tuscan-style wine and food. Cosy up inside its bottle-lined interior or grab a table on the lovely street terrace and dig into Tuscan favourites including crostini (toasts with toppings), *taglieri* (platters of cheese and cured meats), hearty soups, handmade pasta and Florence's iconic T-bone steak. Pizzas are available, too. (06 679 24 70; www.vineriailchianti.com; Via del Lavatore 81-82a; pizzas €8-12, taglieri €14, meals €50; noon-11.30pm; M Barberini)

La Buca di Ripetta

ITALIAN €€

17 MAP P98, A3

Popular with locals, who know a good thing when they taste it, this trattoria serves traditional dishes with a refreshingly refined execution – there's nothing stodgy or overly rich on the menu here. Together, the food, attractive surrounds and friendly service make for an extremely satisfying dining experience. (06 321 93 91; www.labucadiripetta.com/roma; Via di Ripetta 36; meals €45; noon-3.30pm & 7-11pm; M Flaminio)

Babington's Tea Rooms

CAFE €€

18 MAP P98, C3

Founded in 1893 by two English women, these tea rooms were an instant hit with the hordes of English tourists in Rome desperate for a decent cup of tea. Little has changed in the ensuing century and Babington's properly made pots of tea (China, India, Ceylon and herbal), cream teas and dainty finger sandwiches remain its unique selling point. (06 678 60 27; www.babingtons.com; Piazza di Spagna 23; tea menus €17-33; 10am-9.15pm; M Spagna)

Imàgo

ITALIAN €€€

19 MAP P98, D3

Even in a city of great views, the panoramas from Roma Hassler's Michelin-starred romantic rooftop restaurant are special, extending over a sea of roofs to the great dome of St Peter's Basilica; request the corner table. Complementing the views are the bold, modern-Italian creations. (06 6993 4726; www.imagorestaurant.com; Piazza della Trinità dei Monti 6, Roma Hassler; tasting menus €130-170; 7-10.30pm Feb-Dec; ; M Spagna)

Drinking

Zuma Bar

COCKTAIL BAR

20 MAP P98, B4

Dress up for a drink on the rooftop terrace of Palazzo Fendi of fashion-house fame – few cocktail bars in Rome are as sleek, hip or achingly sophisticated as this. City rooftop views are predictably fabulous; cocktails mix exciting flavours like shiso with juniper berries, elderflower and prosecco. DJs spin Zuma playlists at weekends.

(☎06 9926 6622; www.zumarestaurant.com; Via della Fontanella di Borghese 48, Palazzo Fendi; ⏲6pm-1am Sun-Thu, to 2am Fri & Sat; 📶; Ⓜ Spagna)

Antico Caffè Greco

CAFE

21 MAP P98, C4

Rome's oldest cafe, open since 1760, is still working the look with the utmost elegance: waiters in black tails and bow tie or frilly white pinnies, scarlet flock walls and age-spotted gilt mirrors. Prices reflect this amazing heritage: pay €9 for a cappuccino sitting down or join locals for the same (€2.50) standing at the bar. (☎06 679 17 00; www.facebook.com/AnticoCaffeGreco; Via dei Condotti 86; ⏲9am-9pm; Ⓜ Spagna)

Stravinskij Bar

BAR

22 MAP P98, B1

Can't afford to stay at the celeb-magnet **Hotel de Russie** (☎06 32 88 81; www.roccofortehotels.com/it; Via del Babuino 9; d from €600; P ❄ 📶; Ⓜ Flaminio)? Then splash out on a drink at its swish bar. There are sofas inside, but the sunny courtyard is the fashionable choice, with sun-shaded tables overlooked by terraced gardens. Impossibly romantic in the best dolce-vita style, it's perfect for a pricey cocktail or beer accompanied by appropriately posh snacks. (☎06 3288 88 74; www.roccofortehotels.com/hotels-and-resorts/hotel-de-russie/; Via del Babuino 9, Hotel de Russie; ⏲9am-1am; Ⓜ Flaminio)

Sunset Views

One of the best places to catch a memorable Roman view is Piazza del Quirinale in front of the presidential palace on the Quirinal Hill. As the sun dips and the sky takes on a golden, fiery hue, you can gaze over a sea of rooftops to the distant dome of St Peter's Basilica.

Il Palazzetto

COCKTAIL BAR

23 MAP P98, C3

No terrace proffers such a fine view of the Spanish Steps over an expertly shaken cocktail. Ride the lift up from the discreet entrance on narrow Vicolo del Bottino or look for stairs leading to the bar from the top of the steps. Given everything is al fresco, the bar is only open in warm, dry weather. (☎06 6993 4560; Vicolo del Bottino 8; ⏲noon-6pm winter, 4pm-midnight summer, closed in bad weather; Ⓜ Spagna)

Caffè Ciampini

CAFE

24 MAP P98, C3

Hidden away a short walk from the top of the Spanish Steps towards the **Pincio Hill Gardens** (Ⓜ Flaminio), this cafe has a vintage garden-party vibe, with green wooden latticework and orange trees framing its white-clothed tables. There are lovely views over the backstreets behind Spagna,

Passeggiata on Via del Corso

The *passeggiata* (traditional evening stroll) is a quintessential Roman experience. It's particularly colourful at weekends when families, friends and lovers take to the streets to strut up and down, slurp on gelato and window-shop.

To join in, head to Via del Corso around 6pm. Alternatively, park yourself on the Spanish Steps and watch the theatrics unfold beneath you on **Piazza di Spagna** (p96).

and the gelato – particularly the *tartufo al cioccolato* (chocolate truffle) – is renowned. Serves food too. (☎06 678 56 78; Viale Trinità dei Monti; ⏰8am-11pm Mar-Oct; M Spagna)

Bar Frattina CAFE

25 MAP P98, C4

Yes, the Spanish Steps offer a primo people-watching opportunity. But so too does the streetside terrace of this nearby cafe, which has been hugely popular with local workers and residents ever since opening back in the 1950s. Come for coffee or a drink, not to eat. (☎06 679 26 93; www.barfrattina.com; Via Frattina 142; ⏰7am-11pm; M Spagna)

Up Sunset Bar COCKTAIL BAR

26 MAP P98, D5

Perched on the top two floors of luxury department store **La Rinascente** (☎06 87 91 61; www.rinascente.it; Via del Tritone 61; ⏰10am-10pm; 📶; 🚌Via del Corso), this flirty bar promises plenty of champagne, dishes by Michelin-starred chef Riccardo Di Giacinto, and a swish front-row seat to Rome's stunning skyline. Or come in the morning for a cappuccino and *cornetto* (croissant) breakfast with the city sprawled at your feet. (☎06 8791 6652; www.upsunsetbar.com; Via del Tritone 61; ⏰10am-11pm; M Barberini)

Caffè Ripetta CAFE

27 MAP P98, A3

Buzzing with a buoyant, young, staunchly Roman crowd, this sassy corner cafe is a relaxed and easy spot for lapping up a bit of local dolce vita over a love-heart-topped cappuccino. Sit inside at the all-white bar or on the street-smart pavement terrace, heated in winter. Serves pizza (€8.50 to €11) and *panini* (€4.50 to €12) too. (☎06 321 05 24; 39 Via della Frezza; ⏰8.30am-11pm; M Flaminio)

Entertainment

Gregory's Jazz Club JAZZ

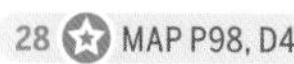

28 MAP P98, D4

If Gregory's were a tone of voice, it'd be husky: unwind over a whisky in the downstairs bar, then unwind some more on squashy sofas upstairs to slinky live jazz and swing, with quality local performers who also like to hang out here. (06 679 63 86, 327 8263770; www.gregorysjazz.com; Via Gregoriana 54d; obligatory drink €15-20; 7.30pm-2am Tue-Sun; ; M Barberini)

Shopping

Bomba

CLOTHING

29 MAP P98, A2

Opened by designer Cristina Bomba over four decades ago, this gorgeous boutique is now operated by her fashion-designing children Caterina (womenswear) and Michele (menswear). Using the highest-quality fabrics, their creations are tailored in the next-door atelier (peek through the front window); woollens are produced at a factory just outside the city. Pricey but oh-so-worth-it. (06 361 28 81; www.cristinabomba.com; Via dell'Oca 39; 11am-7.30pm Tue-Sat, from 3.30pm Mon; M Flaminia)

Gente

FASHION & ACCESSORIES

30 MAP P98, C3

This multi-label boutique was the first in Rome to bring all the big-name luxury designers – Italian, French and otherwise – under one roof, and its vast emporium-styled space remains an essential stop for every serious fashionista. Labels include Dolce & Gabbana, Prada, Alexander McQueen, Sergio Rossi and Missoni. (06 320 76 71; www.genteroma.com; Via del Babuino 77; 10.30am-7.30pm Mon-Fri, to 8pm Sat, 11.30am-7.30pm Sun; M Spagna)

Dresses on display at Gente

Shopping Streets

The Tridente is Rome's premier shopping district. Main drag Via del Corso and the streets surrounding it are lined with flagship stores and beautiful boutiques selling everything from savvy streetwear and haute-couture fashion to handmade paper stationery, artisan jewellery, perfume, homeware and food. Specialist streets include **Via Margutta** (p101) for antiques; **Via dei Condotti** (Map p98, C4; M Spagna), Rome's smartest shopping strip, for designer fashions; and Via della Pugna for small, independent boutiques. Other top addresses include Via Frattina, Via della Croce, Via delle Carrozze and Via del Babuino.

Chiara Baschieri CLOTHING

31 MAP P98, B2

One of Rome's most impressive independent designers, Chiara Baschieri produces classic, meticulously tailored clothing featuring exquisite fabrics. Her style echoes 1960s Givenchy – if Audrey Hepburn had ever stopped by, Chiara would no doubt have gained another fan. (☎333 6364851; www.chiarabaschieri.it; Via Margutta, cnr Vicolo Orto di Napoli; ⏲11am-7pm Tue-Sat; M Spagna)

Fausto Santini SHOES

32 MAP P98, C4

Rome's best-known shoe designer, Fausto Santini is famous for his beguilingly simple, architectural shoe designs, with beautiful boots and shoes made from butter-soft leather. Colours are beautiful, and the quality is impeccable. Seek out the end-of-line **discount shop** (☎06 488 09 34; Via Cavour 106; ⏲10am-1pm & 3.30-7.30pm Mon-Fri, 10am-1.30pm & 3-7.30pm Sat; M Cavour) in Monti to source a bargain – its stock is regularly refreshed. (☎06 678 41 14; www.faustosantini.com; Via Frattina 120; ⏲10am-7.30pm Mon-Sat, 11am-7pm Sun; M Spagna)

Artisanal Cornucopia DESIGN

33 MAP P98, A2

One of several stylish independent boutiques on Via dell'Oca, this chic concept store showcases exclusive handmade pieces by Italian designers: the delicate gold necklaces and other jewellery crafted by Giulia Barela are a highlight, but there are loads of bags, shoes, candles, homewares and other objects to covet. (☎342 8714597; www.artisanalcornucopia.com; Via dell'Oca 38a; ⏲10.30am-7.30pm Tue-Sat, from 3.30pm Mon, from 4.30pm Sun; M Flaminio)

Flumen Profumi PERFUME

34 MAP P98, B4

Unique 'made in Rome' scents are what this artisan perfumery is all about. Natural perfumes are oil-based, contain four to eight base notes and evoke la dolce vita – Incantro fuses pomegranate with white flower, while Ritrovarsi Ancora is a nostalgic fragrance evocative of long, lazy, family meals around a countryside table (smell the fig!). (06 6830 7635; www.flumenprofumi.com; Via della Fontanella di Borghese 41; 11am-2pm & 3.30-7.30pm; Via del Corso)

Anglo American Bookshop BOOKS

35 MAP P98, C4

Particularly good for university reference books, the Anglo American Bookshop is well stocked and well known. It has an excellent range of literature, travel guides, children's books and maps, and if it hasn't got the book you want, staff will order it in. (06 679 52 22; www.aab.it; Via della Vite 102; 10.30am-7.30pm Tue-Sat, from 3.30pm Mon; M Spagna)

Fendi FASHION & ACCESSORIES

36 MAP P98, B4

With travertine walls, stunning contemporary art and sweeping red-marble staircase, the flagship store of Rome's iconic fashion house inside 18th-century Palazzo Fendi is dazzling. Born in Rome in 1925 as a leather and fur workshop on Via del Plebiscit, this luxurious temple to Roman fashion is as much concept store as *maison* selling ready-to-wear clothing for men and women. (06 3345 0890; www.fendi.com; Largo Carlo Goldoni 420, Palazzo Fendi; 10am-7.30pm Mon-Sat, from 10.30am Sun; M Spagna)

Federico Buccellati JEWELLERY

37 MAP P98, C4

Run today by the third generation of one of Italy's most prestigious silver- and goldsmiths, this historical shop opened in 1926. Everything is handcrafted and often delicately engraved with decorative flowers, leaves and nature-inspired motifs. Don't miss the Silver Salon on the 1st floor showcasing some original silverware and jewellery pieces by grandfather Mario. (06 679 03 29; www.facebook.com/federico-buccellati-orafo-311172238241; Via dei Condotti 31; 10am-1.30pm & 3-7pm Tue-Fri, 10am-1.30pm & 2-6pm Sat, 3-7pm Mon; M Spagna)

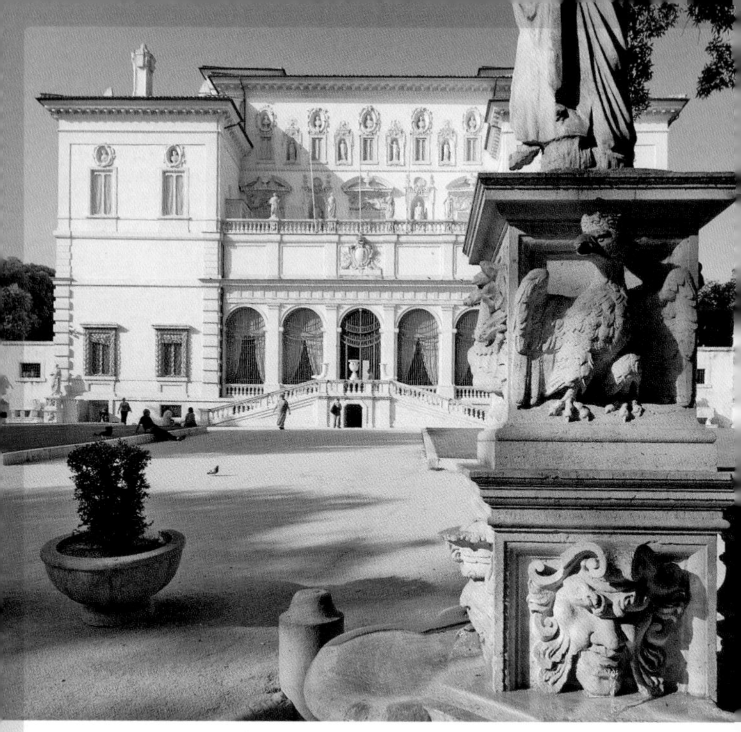

Worth a Trip

Admire the artworks at Museo e Galleria Borghese

If you only have the time or inclination for one art gallery in Rome, make it this one. Housing what's often referred to as the 'queen of all private art collections', it holds some of the city's finest art treasures, including a series of sensational sculptures by Gian Lorenzo Bernini and important paintings by the likes of Caravaggio, Titian, Raphael and Rubens.

06 3 28 10

http://galleriaborghese.beniculturali.it

Piazzale del Museo Borghese 5

adult/reduced €15/8.50

9am-7pm Tue-Sun

Via Pinciana

The Villa

The museum's collection was formed by Cardinal Scipione Borghese (1577–1633), the most knowledgeable and ruthless art collector of his day. It was originally housed in the cardinal's residence near St Peter's, but in the 1620s he had it transferred to his new villa just outside Porta Pinciana. And it's in the villa's central building, the Casino Borghese, that you'll see it today.

The villa is divided into two parts: the ground-floor museum, with its superb sculptures, Roman floor mosaics and trompe l'œil frescoes; and the upstairs picture gallery.

Ground Floor

Stairs lead up to a portico flanking the grand entrance hall, decorated with 4th-century floor mosaics of fighting gladiators and a 2nd-century *Satiro Combattente* (Fighting Satyr). High on the wall is a gravity-defying bas-relief of a horse and rider falling into the void *(Marco Curzio a Cavallo)* by Pietro Bernini (Gian Lorenzo's father).

The statuesque scene-stealer in **Sala I** is Antonio Canova's daring depiction of Napoleon's sister, Paolina Bonaparte Borghese, reclining topless as *Venere vincitrice* (1805–08).

Further on, in **Sala III**, Bernini's *Apollo e Dafne* (1622–25), one of a series depicting pagan myths, captures the exact moment Daphne's hands start morphing into leaves. **Sala IV** is home to Bernini's masterpiece *Ratto di Proserpina* (1621–22), which brilliantly reveals the artist's virtuosity – just look at Pluto's hand pressing into the seemingly soft flesh of Persephone's thigh.

Caravaggio dominates **Sala VIII**. There's a dissipated-looking self-portrait *Bacchino malato* (Young Sick Bacchus; 1592–95), the strangely beautiful *La Madonna dei Palafrenieri* (Madonna with Serpent; 1605–06), and *San*

★ Top Tips

- To limit numbers, visitors are admitted at two-hourly intervals – book your ticket well in advance and get an entry time.
- To book, phone the museum directly or buy tickets at www.tosc.it.
- Pick up your ticket from the ticket office 30 minutes before your entry time. Take ID.

✕ Take a Break

Head through Villa Borghese to the **Caffè delle Arti** (☎06 3265 1236; www.caffedelleartiroma.com; Via Gramsci 73; meals €40-45; ⏲8am-5pm Mon, 8am-midnight Tue-Sun; 🚊Piazza Thorvaldsen), a grand cafe-restaurant serving coffee and meals at La Galleria Nazionale.

★ Getting There

🚌 Bus 53 or 910 to Via Pinciana.

Ⓜ From Spagna (line A) you can walk up to Villa Borghese.

Giovanni Battista (St John the Baptist; 1609–10), probably Caravaggio's last work. There's also the much-loved *Ragazzo col Canestro di Frutta* (Boy with a Basket of Fruit; 1593–95), and the dramatic *Davide con la Testa di Golia* (David with the Head of Goliath; 1609–10) – Goliath's severed head is also said to be a self-portrait.

Pinacoteca

Upstairs, the picture gallery offers a wonderful snapshot of Renaissance art. Don't miss Raphael's extraordinary *La Deposizione di Cristo* (The Deposition; 1507) in **Sala IX**, and his *Dama con Liocorno* (Lady with a Unicorn; 1506). In the same room is Fra Bartolomeo's superb *Adorazione del Bambino* (Adoration of the Christ Child; 1495) and Perugino's *Madonna con Bambino* (Madonna and Child; first quarter of the 16th century).

Next door in **Sala X**, Correggio's *Danäe* (1530–31) shares the room with a willowy Venus, as portrayed by Cranach in his *Venere e Amore che Reca Il Favo do Miele* (Venus and Cupid with Honeycomb; 1531).

Moving on, **Sala XVIII** is home to Rubens' *Susanna e I Vecchioni* (Susanna and the Elders; 1605–07).

To finish off, Titian's early masterpiece *Amor Sacro e Amor Profano* (Sacred and Profane Love; 1514), in **Sala XX**, is one of the collection's most prized works.

Villa Borghese

Extending for about 80 hectares around the Museo, **Villa Borghese** (entrances at Piazzale San Paolo del Brasile, Piazzale Flaminio, Via Pinciana, Via Raimondo, Largo Pablo Picasso; sunrise-sunset; Via Pinciana) is Rome's Central Park, a verdant oasis of wooded glades, gardens and grassy banks.

Among its attractions are two excellent museums: the **Museo Nazionale Etrusco di Villa Giulia** (06 322 65 71; www.villagiulia.beniculturali.it; Piazzale di Villa Giulia; adult/reduced €8/4; 9am-8pm Tue-Sun; Via delle Belle Arti), showcasing Italy's finest collection of Etruscan and pre-Roman treasures, and **La Galleria Nazionale** (Galleria Nazionale d'Arte Moderna e Contemporanea; 06 3229 8221; http://lagallerianazionale.com; Viale delle Belle Arti 131, accessible entrance Via Antonio Gramsci 71; adult/reduced €10/5; 8.30am-7.30pm Tue-Sun; Piazza Thorvaldsen), with a superlative collection of modern art.

Auditorium Parco della Musica

The hub of Rome's cultural scene, the **Auditorium Parco della Musica** (06 8024 1281; www.auditorium.com; Viale Pietro de Coubertin; Viale Tiziano) is the capital's premier concert venue. Its three concert halls and 3000-seat open-air arena stage everything from classical music concerts to jazz gigs, public lectures and film screenings.

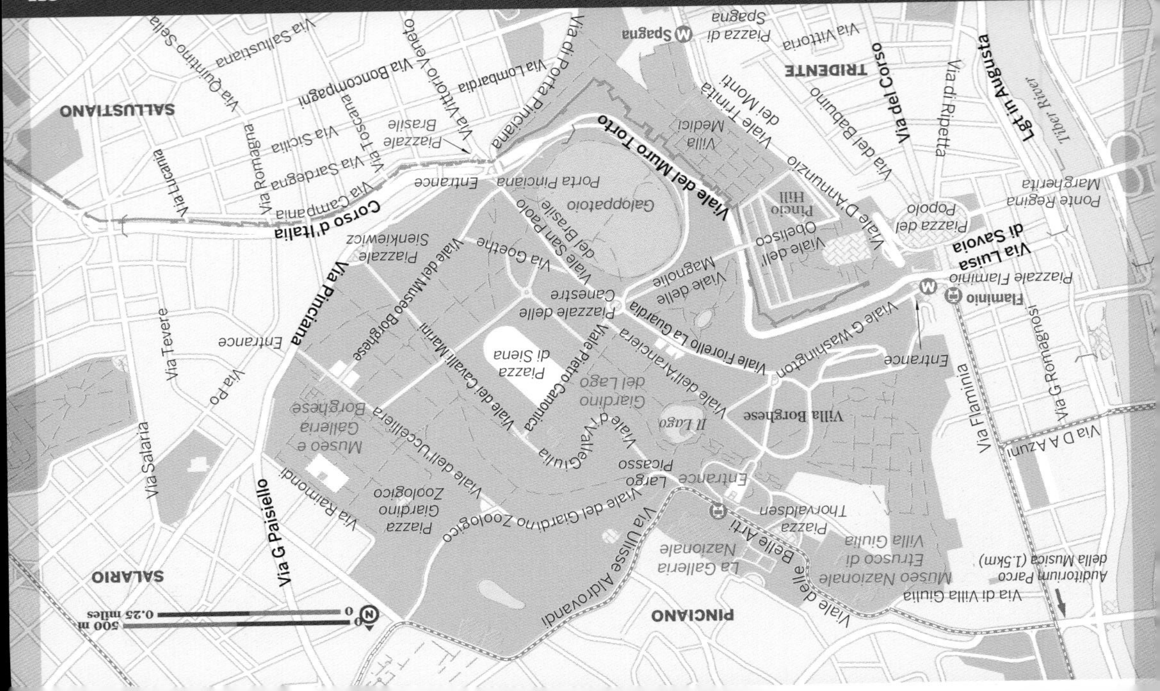

SALUSTIANO
SALARIO
PINCIANO
TRIDENTE
Via G Paisiello
Via Salaria
Via Tevere
Via Po
Via Lucania
Via Romagna
Via Quintino Sella
Via Sallustiana
Via Boncompagni
Via Sicilia
Via Sardegna
Via Campania
Via Toscana
Piazzale Brasile
Via Vittorio Veneto
Via Lombardia
Via di Porta Pinciana
Corso d'Italia
Via Pinciana
Entrance
Piazzale Sienkiewicz
Viale del Museo Borghese
Viale dei Cavalli Marini
Via Goethe
Viale San Paolo del Brasile
Galoppatoio
Porta Pinciana
Viale del Muro Torto
Villa Medici
Viale Trinita dei Monti
Piazza di Spagna
Spagna
Via Vittoria
Via del Babuino
Via del Corso
Via di Ripetta
Lgt in Augusta
Tiber River
Ponte Regina Margherita
Piazza del Popolo
Viale D'Annunzio
Pincio Hill
Viale dell' Obelisco
Viale delle Magnolie
Piazzale delle Canestre
Viale Fiorello La Guardia
Viale dell'Aranciera
Viale Pietro Canonica
Piazza di Siena
Giardino del Lago
Il Lago
Viale d. Valle Giulia
Largo Picasso
Villa Borghese
Viale G Washington
Via Luisa di Savoia
Piazzale Flaminio
Flaminio
Via Flaminia
Via G Romagnosi
Via D A Azuni
Museo e Galleria Borghese
Via Raimondi
Piazza Giardino Zoologico
Viale dell'Uccelliera
Viale del Giardino Zoologico
Via Ulisse Aldrovandi
La Galleria Nazionale
Viale delle Belle Arti
Piazza Thorvaldsen
Museo Nazionale Etrusco di Villa Giulia
Via di Villa Giulia
Auditorium Parco della Musica (1.5km)
0 500 m
0 0.25 miles

Explore

Monti & Esquilino

Centred on transport hub Stazione Termini, this is a large and cosmopolitan area which, upon first glance, can seem busy and overwhelming. But hidden among its traffic-noisy streets are some beautiful churches, Rome's best unsung art museum at Palazzo Massimo alle Terme, and any number of trendy bars and restaurants in the fashionable Monti district.

The Short List

- ***Palazzo Massimo alle Terme (p118)*** *Evoking the ancient past when viewing exquisite frescoes from villas of imperial Rome at one of the city's finest museums.*
- ***Monti (p120)*** *Pottering around Rome's romantic, bohemian-chic neighbourhood, lingering at wine bars, sipping coffee on pavement terraces and browsing artisan boutiques.*
- ***Basilica di Santa Maria Maggiore (p123)*** *Marvelling at the Byzantine and baroque splendours of one of Rome's four patriarchal basilicas.*
- ***Domus Aurea (p124)*** *Exploring the subterranean remains of Nero's massive golden palace.*

Getting There & Around

M Cavour (line B) for Monti; Termini (lines A and B), Castro Pretorio (line B) and Vittorio Emanuele (line A) are all useful for Esquilino.

Bus: Termini is the main hub, connected to places all over the city. Access Monti from buses stopping on Via Nazionale or Via Cavour.

Monti & Esquilino Map on p122

Basilica di Santa Maria Maggiore (p123) ESSEVU / GETTY IMAGES ©

Top Experience

Peruse the treasures of Palazzo Massimo alle Terme

One of Rome's finest museums, this often empty branch of the Museo Nazionale is packed with spectacular classical art. Start your visit on the 2nd floor, so as to see its wonders when you're fresh – the frescoes and mosaics here offer a scintillating evocation of what the interiors of grand ancient Roman villas looked like.

MAP P122, D2

www.coopculture.it

Largo di Villa Peretti 1

adult/reduced €10/5

9am-7.45pm Tue-Sun

M Termini

Villa Livia Frescoes

The 2nd-floor showstopper is Room 2, where frescoes from Villa Livia, one of the homes of Augustus' wife Livia Drusilla, are displayed. These decorated a summer triclinium, a large living and dining area built half underground to provide protection from the heat, and depict a lush garden under a deep-blue, bird-filled sky. The 1st-century BC villa was rediscovered in 1863 after being abandoned around the 5th century AD.

Villa Farnesina Frescoes

Frescoes and intricate mosaic floors from the Villa Farnesina are also displayed on the 2nd floor (Rooms 3 to 5). The villa was home to General Marcus Vipsanius Agrippa, a close friend of Augustus. There are friezes of caryatids (sculpted female figures serving as an architectural support); frescoed still lifes; and bedrooms decorated with images of the goddesses Artemis and Aphrodite. A multimedia presentation gives an excellent idea of what the villa, which was rediscovered in Trastevere in 1879, would have looked like.

Ground & 1st Floors

The ground and 1st floors are devoted to sculpture. On the 1st floor, don't miss a mid-3rd-century BC marble statue known as the *Anzio Maiden,* which depicts a young girl participating in a Dionysian Ritual (Room 6). On the ground floor, the highlights are two 2nd-century-BC Greek bronzes, *The Boxer* and *The Prince* (Room 7); and the 4th-century-BC marble *Dying Niobid* statue in Room 6.

Basement

In the basement, the coin collection is far more absorbing than you might expect, tracing the history of the Roman Empire via coinage.

★ Top Tips

- Rent an audio guide at the main ticket desk for €5.
- Combination tickets, valid for three days, also cover the Museo Nazionale Romano's other seats at: Terme di Diocleziano (p124), Palazzo Altemps (p62) and **Crypta Balbi**.

✕ Take a Break

Whatever the time of day, the food stalls at Mercato Centrale (p126) offer up almost every popular edible under the Roman sun.

To enjoy a coffee and decadently sweet Sicilian pastry, make the short walk to Dagnino (p128) in the nearby Esedra Arcade.

Walking Tour

Bars & Boutiques in Monti

The first residential rione *(district) established beyond the walls of the imperial city, Monti was once a working class area infamous for its brothels, seedy wine shops and general air of debauchery. These days, the brothels have been replaced by artisanal boutiques, the wine shops have morphed into bohemian bars and the ambience is local, arty and pretension-free.*

Walk Facts

Start La Bottega del Caffè; metro Cavour

End Blackmarket Hall; metro Cavour

Length 1.9km; one day

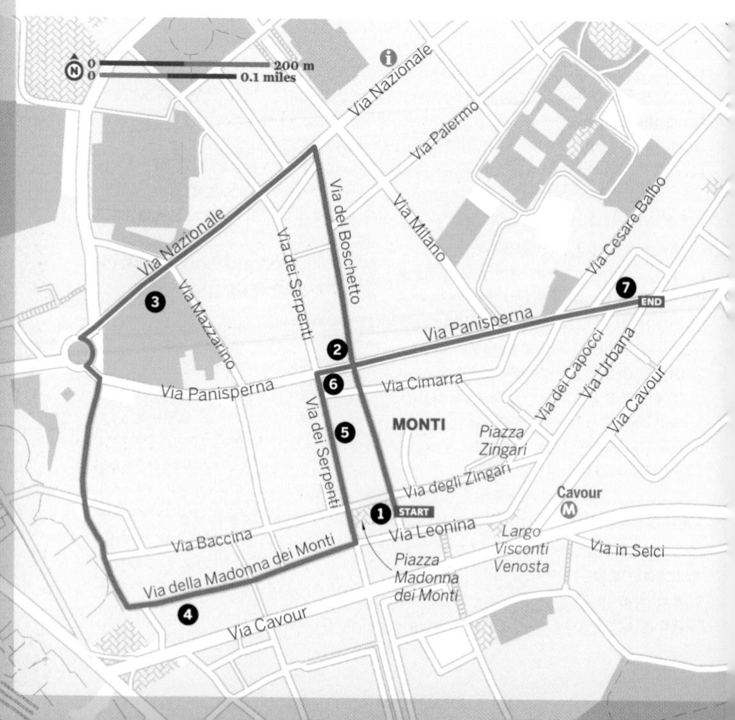

❶ Morning Coffee

Set on the eastern edge of pocket-sized Piazza della Madonna dei Monti with its pretty Fontana dei Catecumeni, a fountain named for adults initiated to the Catholic Church, **La Bottega del Caffè** (p128) serves the best coffee in Monti, and also has the most alluring terrace. Colonise a table and watch local life unfold in front of you.

❷ Via del Boschetto

Sauntering along this street proves that Monti's much-hyped reputation as an alternative fashion hub is fully justified. Clothing boutiques such as **Tina Sondergaard** (p129) have led the way, joined by vintage outlets, jewellery stores and other tempting businesses.

❸ Villa Aldobrandini

During the high season Monti can be a maelstrom of crowds, so it's a relief to know that there is a tranquil bolthole available just off traffic-choked Via Nazionale. This sculpture-dotted **garden** (p125) in front of a 16th-century villa has a scattering of benches beneath perfumed orange trees, where it's easy to catch one's breath.

❹ Pizza Refuel

Every neighbourhood needs a welcoming pizzeria, and Monti has one of the best in town. **Alle Carrette** (p125) serves up thin-crust, piping-hot pizza to a constant stream of locals and tourists, and is just as popular at lunch as it is later in the evening. Sit inside in winter and in the rear laneway during the warmer months.

❺ Via dei Serpenti

Another excellent shopping street, Via dei Serpenti has a view of the Colosseum from its southern end and a garland of tempting boutiques stretching north on each side of the road, including one of the city's best vintage clothing shops, **Pifebo** (p129).

❻ Ai Tre Scalini

A popular local hang-out since 1895, **To The Three Steps** (p127) is perennially packed with young Romans – many local – who catch up with friends over beers, glasses of wine and generous cheese and *salumi* platters. Those who can't cram in often adjourn to **Barzilai Bistro** (p128), opposite.

❼ Into the Wee Hours

Monti has more than its fair share of bars, all with their own character. Multi-roomed speakeasy **Blackmarket Hall** (p127) is popular with locals who want to enjoy a quiet drink and conversation rather than hang out in one of the noisy local wine bars. The volume picks up at weekends, though, when live music acts perform.

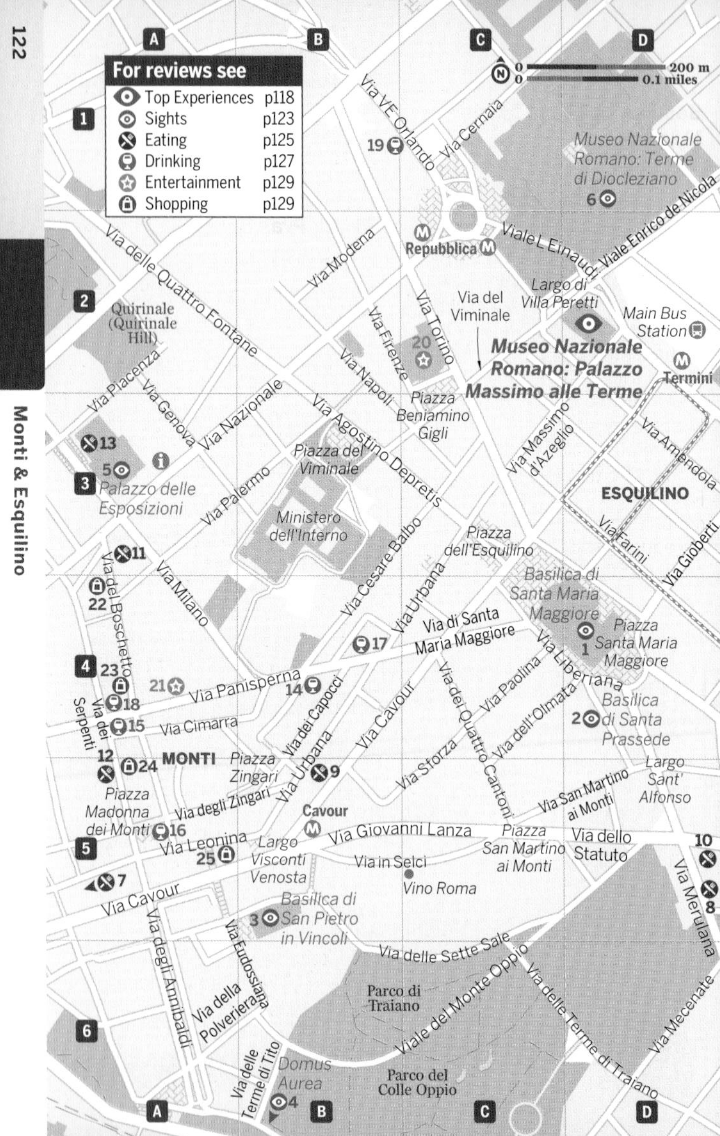
For reviews see
Top Experiences p118
Sights p123
Eating p125
Drinking p127
Entertainment p129
Shopping p129
A
B
C
D
1
2
3
4
5
6
0 200 m
0 0.1 miles
Via VE Orlando
Via Cernaia
Museo Nazionale Romano: Terme di Diocleziano
6
Viale Enrico de Nicola
Viale L Einaudi
Repubblica
Largo di Villa Peretti
Main Bus Station
Via del Viminale
Museo Nazionale Romano: Palazzo Massimo alle Terme
Termini
Via delle Quattro Fontane
Quirinale (Quirinale Hill)
Via Modena
Via Torino
Via Firenze
20
Via Napoli
Piazza Beniamino Gigli
Via Piacenza
Via Genova
Via Nazionale
Via Agostino Depretis
Via Massimo d'Azeglio
Via Amendola
ESQUILINO
13
5
Palazzo delle Esposizioni
Via Palermo
Piazza del Viminale
Ministero dell'Interno
Via Cesare Balbo
Piazza dell'Esquilino
Via Farini
Via Gioberti
11
Via del Boschetto
22
Via Milano
Basilica di Santa Maria Maggiore
Via Urbana
Via di Santa Maria Maggiore
17
1
Piazza Santa Maria Maggiore
Via Liberiana
23
21
Via Panisperna
14
Via dei Capocci
Via Cavour
Via dei Quattro Cantoni
Via Paolina
Via dell'Olmata
Basilica di Santa Prassede
2
18
Via dei Serpenti
15
Via Cimarra
12
24
MONTI
Piazza Zingari
Via Urbana
9
Via Sforza
Largo Sant' Alfonso
Via San Martino ai Monti
Piazza Madonna dei Monti
Via degli Zingari
Cavour
16
Via Leonina
25
Largo Visconti Venosta
Via Giovanni Lanza
Piazza San Martino ai Monti
Via dello Statuto
10
Via in Selci
Vino Roma
7
Via Cavour
Via Merulana
8
Basilica di San Pietro in Vincoli
3
Via degli Annibaldi
Via Eudossiana
Via delle Sette Sale
Via del Monte Oppio
Via delle Terme di Traiano
Parco di Traiano
Via della Polveriera
Viale del Monte Oppio
Via Mecenate
Via delle Terme di Tito
Domus Aurea
4
Parco del Colle Oppio

Sights

Basilica di Santa Maria Maggiore BASILICA

1 MAP P122, D4

One of Rome's four patriarchal basilicas, this 5th-century church stands on Esquiline Hill's summit, on the spot where snow is said to have miraculously fallen in the summer of AD 358. Every year on 5 August the event is recreated during a light show in Piazza Santa Maria Maggiore. Much altered over the centuries, the basilica is an architectural hybrid with 14th-century Romanesque campanile, Renaissance coffered ceiling, 18th-century baroque facade, largely baroque interior and a series of glorious 5th-century mosaics. (06 6988 6800; Piazza Santa Maria Maggiore; basilica free, adult/reduced museum €3/2, loggia €5; 7am-6.45pm, loggia guided tours 9.30am-5.45pm; M Termini or Cavour)

Basilica di Santa Prassede CHURCH

2 MAP P122, D4

Famous for its Byzantine mosaics, which have been preserved in their original state, this small 9th-century church is dedicated to St Praxedes, an early Christian heroine who hid Christians fleeing persecution and buried those she couldn't save in a well. The position of the well is now marked by a marble disc on the floor of the nave. (Via Santa Prassede 9a; 7am-noon & 4-6.30pm; M Cavour)

Stained glass window, Basilica di Santa Maria Maggiore. Artist: Giovanni Hajnal

Basilica di San Pietro in Vincoli BASILICA

3 MAP P122, B5

Pilgrims and art lovers flock to this 5th-century basilica for two reasons: to marvel at Michelangelo's colossal *Moses* sculpture (1505) and to see the chains that are said to have bound St Peter when he was imprisoned in the Carcere Mamertino ('in Vincoli' means 'in Chains'). Also of note is a lovely 7th-century mosaic icon of St Sebastian. Access to the church is via a steep flight of steps leading up from Via Cavour and passing under a low arch. (06 9784 4950; Piazza di San Pietro in Vincoli 4a; 8am-12.20pm & 3-6.50pm summer, to 5.50pm winter; M Cavour)

Domus Aurea ARCHAEOLOGICAL SITE

4 MAP P122, B6

Nero had his Domus Aurea constructed after the fire of AD 64 (which he is rumoured to have started to clear the area). Named after the gold that lined its facade and interiors, it was a huge complex covering almost one third of the city. Making some use of video and virtual reality, multi-language guided tours of its ruins shed light on how it would have appeared in its prime. Advance online reservations (€2) are obligatory. Enter from Via Labicana. (Golden House; 06 3996 7700; www.coopculture.it; Viale della Domus Aurea, Parco del Colle Oppio; adult/under 6yr €14/free; 9.15am-4.15pm Sat & Sun; M Colosseo)

Palazzo delle Esposizioni CULTURAL CENTRE

5 MAP P122, A3

This huge neoclassical palace was built in 1882 as an exhibition centre, though it has since served as headquarters for the Italian Communist Party, a mess hall for Allied servicemen, a polling station and even a public loo. Nowadays it's a splendid cultural hub, with cathedral-scale exhibition spaces hosting blockbuster art exhibitions and sleekly designed art labs, as well as an upmarket restaurant (p126) serving dinner and a bargain-priced weekday lunch or weekend brunch buffet beneath a dazzling all-glass roof. (06 3996 7500; www.palazzoesposizioni.it; Via Nazionale 194; 10am-8pm Tue-Thu & Sun, to 10.30pm Fri & Sat; Via Nazionale)

Museo Nazionale Romano: Terme di Diocleziano MUSEUM

6 MAP P122, D1

Able to accommodate some 3000 people, the Terme di Diocleziano was ancient Rome's largest bath complex. Now an epigraphic museum, its exhibits provide a fascinating insight into ancient Roman life, with the highlight being the upstairs exhibition relating to cults. There's also a temporary exhibition area in the massive baths hall and a 16th-century cloister that was built as part of the charterhouse of **Santa Maria degli Angeli e dei Martiri** (06 488 08

12; www.santamariadegliangeliroma.it; Piazza della Repubblica; 7.30am-6.30pm Mon-Sat, to 8pm Sun; M Repubblica). The cloister's design was based on drawings by Michelangelo. (06 3996 7700; www.coopculture.it; Viale Enrico de Nicola 78; adult/reduced €10/5; 9am-6.30pm Tue-Sun; M Termini)

Eating

Alle Carrette — PIZZA €

7 MAP P122, A5

Authentic pizza, super-thin and swiftly cooked in a wood-burning oven, is what this traditional Roman pizzeria on one of Monti's prettiest streets has done well for decades. Romans pile in here at weekends for good reason – it's cheap, friendly and delicious. All of the classic toppings are available, as well as gourmet choices such as anchovy and zucchini flower (yum!). (06 679 27 70; www.facebook.com/allecarrette; Via della Madonna dei Monti 95; pizza €5.50-9; 11.30am-4pm & 7pm-midnight; M Cavour)

Panella — BAKERY €

8 MAP P122, D5

Freshly baked pastries, fruit tartlets, *pizza al taglio* (pizza by the slice) and focaccia fill display cases in this famous bakery, and there's also a *tavola calda* ('hot table') where an array of hot dishes are on offer. Order at the counter and eat at bar stools between shelves of gourmet groceries, or sit on the terrace for waiter service. (06 487 24 35; www.panellaroma.com; Via Merulana 54; meals €7-15; 7am-11pm Mon-Thu & Sun, to midnight Fri & Sat; M Vittorio Emanuele)

Villa Aldobrandini

If you're in need of a breather around Via Nazionale or are in search of somewhere for a picnic, follow Via Mazzarino off the main road and walk up the steps, past 2nd-century ruins, to **Villa Aldobrandini** (Via Mazzarino; dawn-dusk; Via Nazionale), a graceful, sculpture-dotted garden with gravel paths and benches beneath fragrant orange trees, palms and camellias.

Zia Rosetta — SANDWICHES €

9 MAP P122, B5

Grab a pew at a marble-topped table and brace your taste buds for a torturous choice between 25-odd gourmet *panini* and another dozen specials – all creatively stuffed with unexpected combinations, and with catchy names like Amber Queen, Strawberry Hill and Lady Godiva. If you really can't decide, pick a trio of mini *panini*. Freshly squeezed juices are €3.50. (06 3105 2516; www.ziarosetta.com; Via Urbana 54; salads €6-8, panini mini €2-3.50, regular €4.50-7; 11am-4pm Mon-Thu, to 10pm Fri-Sun; M Cavour)

Termini Food Hall

A gourmet food hall for hungry travellers at Stazione Termini, the **Mercato Centrale** (www.mercatocentrale.it/roma; Stazione Termini, Via Giolitti 36; snacks/meals from €3/10; 8am-midnight; ; M Termini), with its vaulted 1930s ceiling, hosts stalls selling good-quality fast food and fresh produce. Consider purchasing a *panino* filled with artisanal cheese from Beppe Giovali; a slice of focaccia or pizza from Gabriele Bonci; or a Chianina burger from Enrico Lagorio. A *birreria* (beer house) sells craft beer.

Pasticceria Regoli

BAKERY €

10 MAP P122, D5

At weekends a queue marks the entrance to this elegant chandelier-lit *pasticceria*, much loved since 1916. Its *crostate* (latticed jam tarts) are iconic, as are its berry-topped *crostatine fragoline di bosco*. Take a number from the machine next to the register, order when it's called and then pay. (06 487 28 12; www.pasticceriaregoli.com; Via dello Statuto 60; cakes €6; cafe 6.30am-6.45pm Wed-Mon, shop to 8.20pm; M Vittorio Emanuele)

La Barrique

ITALIAN €€

11 MAP P122, A3

This traditional *enoteca* is a classy yet casual place to linger over a meal. There's a large wine list, mostly sourced from small producers, with lots of natural wines to choose from. A small menu of creative pastas and mains provides a great accompaniment – this is one of the best places to eat in Monti. Bookings recommended. (06 4782 5953; www.facebook.com/la.barrique.94/; Via del Boschetto 41b; meals €40; 1-2.30pm & 7.30-11pm Mon-Fri, 7.30-11.30pm Sat; M Cavour)

Temakinho

SUSHI €€

12 MAP P122, A5

In a city where most food is still resolutely (though deliciously) Italian, this branch of a chain of Brazilian-Japanese hybrid restaurants makes for a refreshing change. As well as sushi and ceviche, it serves delicious, strong *caipirinha* cocktails, which combine Brazilian *cachaça*, sugar, lime and fresh fruit; there are also 'sakehinhas' made with sake. It's very popular so book ahead. (06 4201 6656; www.temakinho.com; Via dei Serpenti 16; dishes €8-15; 12.30-3.30pm & 7pm-midnight; ; M Cavour)

Antonello Colonna Open

GASTRONOMY €€€

13 MAP P122, A3

Spectacularly set at the back of the Palazzo delle Esposizioni (p124), Antonello Colonna's restaurant lounges dramatically under a dazzling all-glass roof. Cuisine is new Roman – innovative takes on traditional dishes, cooked with wit and flair. On sunny days, dine alfresco on the rooftop terrace. The all-you-can-eat weekday lunch buffet and weekend brunch are cheap but unremarkable. (06 4782 2641; www.antonellocolonna.it; Via Milano 9a; lunch/brunch €16/30, à la carte meals €80-100; 12.30-3.30pm & 7-11pm Tue-Sat, 12.30-3.30pm Sun; ; M Repubblica)

Drinking

Blackmarket Hall

COCKTAIL BAR

14 MAP P122, B4

One of Monti's best bars, this multi-roomed speakeasy in a former monastery has an eclectic vintage-style decor and plenty of cosy corners where you can enjoy a leisurely, convivial drink. It serves food up till midnight (burgers €12 to €15) and hosts live music – often jazz – on weekends. There's a second venue nearby on Via Panisperna 101. (339 7351926; www.facebook.com/blackmarkethall/; Via de Ciancaleoni 31; 6pm-3am; M Cavour)

Ai Tre Scalini

WINE BAR

15 MAP P122, A4

A firm favourite since 1895, the 'Three Steps' is always packed, with predominantly young patrons spilling out of its bar area and into the street. It's a perfect spot to enjoy an afternoon drink or a simple meal of cheese, salami and dishes such as *polpette al sugo* (meatballs with sauce), washed down with superb choices of wine or beer. (06 4890 7495; www.facebook.com/aitrescalini; Via Panisperna 251; 12.30pm-1am; M Cavour)

Mercato Centrale

Wine Tasting

With beautifully appointed century-old cellars and a chic tasting studio, **Vino Roma** (Map p122, C5; ☎328 4874497; www.vinoroma.com; Via in Selci 84g; 2-hr tastings per person €50; Ⓜ Cavour) guides both novices and wine enthusiasts in the basics of Italian wine under the knowledgeable stewardship of sommelier Hande Leimer and her expert team. Also on offer are a wine-and-cheese dinner (€60) with snacks and cold cuts to accompany the wines, and bespoke three-hour food tours. Book online.

La Bottega del Caffè

CAFE

16 MAP P122, A5

On one of Rome's prettiest squares in Monti, La Bottega del Caffè – named after a comedy by Carlo Goldoni – is the hot spot in Monti for lingering over excellent coffee, drinks, snacks and lunch or dinner. Heaters in winter ensure balmy alfresco action year-round. (☎06 474 15 78; Piazza Madonna dei Monti 5; ⏲8am-2am; 📶; Ⓜ Cavour)

Blackmarket 101

BAR

17 MAP P122, B4

Filled with vintage sofas and armchairs, this hipster-ish bar with its living-room vibe pours craft beer and cocktails, and stages acoustic live gigs in the intimate back room (cover usually €10). (☎339 8227541; www.facebook.com/blackmarketmont/; Via Panisperna 101; ⏲7pm-2am; Ⓜ Cavour)

Barzilai Bistro

BAR

18 MAP P122, A4

Opposite Monti's much-loved Ai Tre Scalini (p127), this bohemian bar-bistro accommodates the people who can't squeeze in over the road but are seeking a similarly casual place to enjoy a drink and something to eat. Sit at one of the tables under the huge chandelier or stand at the bar; when it's full, they're happy to serve your drinks through the window. (☎06 487 49 79; Via Panisperna 44; ⏲5.30pm-midnight; Ⓜ Cavour)

Dagnino

CAFE

19 MAP P122, B1

Secreted in the Esedra Arcade near Piazza della Repubblica, this cafe has retained its original 1960s decor, including murals – you'll feel like you're entering a time-warp when enjoying a coffee and one of the Sicilian-style treats (*cannoli*, *cassatas* etc) displayed in the long display case. The gelato here is also good. (☎06 481 86 60; Via Vittorio Emanuele Orlando 75; ⏲7am-11pm; Ⓜ Repubblica)

Entertainment

Teatro dell'Opera di Roma
OPERA

20 MAP P122, C2

Rome's premier opera house boasts a dramatic red-and-gold interior, a Fascist 1920s exterior and an impressive history: it premiered both Puccini's *Tosca* and Mascagni's *Cavalleria rusticana*. Opera and ballet performances are staged between November and June. (06 48 16 01; www.operaroma.it; Piazza Beniamino Gigli 1; box office 10am-6pm Mon-Sat, 9am-1.30pm Sun; M Repubblica)

Charity Café
LIVE MUSIC

21 MAP P122, A4

A narrow space, spindly tables, dim lighting and laid-back vibe: this is a place to snuggle down and listen to some slinky live jazz or blues. Gigs usually take place from 10pm; *aperitivo* is between 6pm and 9pm. Check the website to see who's performing. It's closed on Sundays in summer. (06 4782 5881; www.charitycafe.it; Via Panisperna 68; 6pm-2am Tue-Sun; M Cavour)

Shopping

Perlei
JEWELLERY

22 MAP P122, A4

Pieces of avant-garde body jewellery catch the eye in the window of this tiny artisan jeweller on Monti's best shopping street. Inside, handmade pieces by Tammar Edelman and Elinor Avni will appeal to those with a modernist aesthetic. (06 4891 3862; www.perlei.com; Via del Boschetto 35; 10am-8pm Mon-Sat, 11am-2pm & 3-7pm Sun; M Cavour)

Tina Sondergaard
FASHION

23 MAP P122, A4

Sublimely cut and retro-esque, Tina Sondergaard's handmade creations for women are a hit with the local fashion cognoscenti. Styles change by the week rather than the season, femininity is the leitmotif, and you can have adjustments made. (06 8365 57 61; www.facebook.com/tina.sondergaard.rome; Via del Boschetto 1d; 10.30am-7.30pm Mon-Sat, closed Aug; M Cavour)

Pifebo
VINTAGE

24 MAP P122, A5

Grab a secondhand steal at Rome's top vintage boutique. Shelves and racks brim with boots, clothing, bags and an impressive sports jersey collection, all hailing from the '70s, '80s and '90s. (06 8901 5204; www.pifebo.com; Via dei Serpenti 141; 11am-3pm & 4-8pm Mon-Sat, noon-8pm Sun; ; M Cavour)

Mercato Monti Market
MARKET

25 MAP P122, A5

Vintage clothes, accessories, one-off pieces by local designers; this market in the hip 'hood of Monti is well worth a rummage if you're here on a weekend. (www.mercatomonti.com; Via Leonina 46; 10am-8pm Sat & Sun Sep-Jun; M Cavour)

Walking Tour

Hanging Out in San Lorenzo

The presence of the huge Sapienza University of Rome, founded way back in 1303, gives this area immediately southeast of Termini Station a lively feel, with bars, clubs and budget eateries solidly geared towards students. It's also popular with left-wing bohemian types, who patronise the art galleries, cultural centres and performance venues found on almost every graffiti-clad street.

Getting There

A short walk from Termini Station

Catch tram 19 or 3

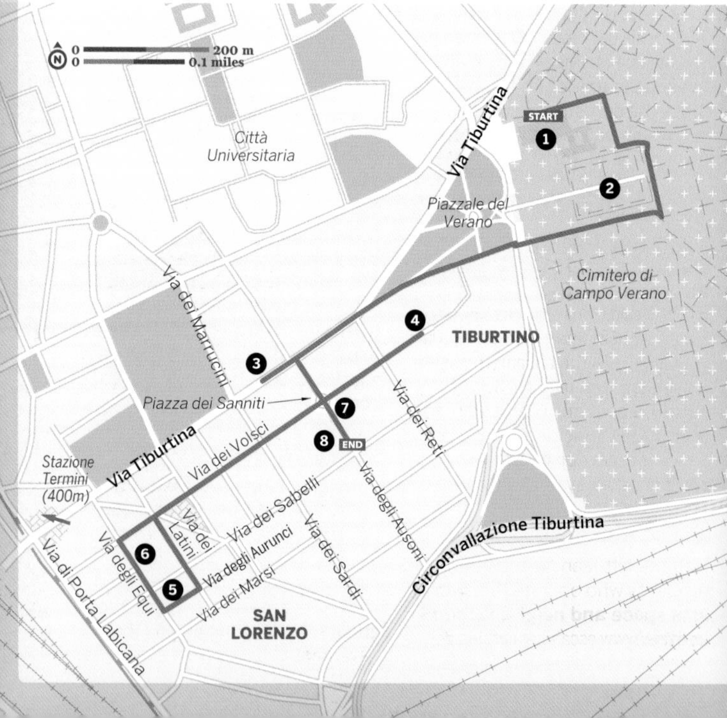

❶ Basilica di San Lorenzo Fuori le Mura

Standing on the site of St Lawrence's burial place, this **basilica** (Piazzale San Lorenzo; ⏲8am-noon & 4-6.30pm; 🚌Piazzale del Verano) suffered bomb damage in WWII but retains a stunning Cosmati floor and 13th-century frescoed portico.

❷ Explore the Cimitero di Campo Verano

The **Cimitero di Campo Verano** (www.cimitericapitolini.it; Piazzale del Verano 1; ⏲7.30am-6pm Apr-Sep, to 5pm Oct-Dec, to 1pm Jan-Mar; 🚌Piazzale del Verano, 🚋Piazzale del Verano) is a strangely moving place. Avenues of grandiose tombs crisscross the cemetery, Rome's largest, which dates to the Napoleonic occupation of Rome (1804–14).

❸ Chocolate Stop

Sightseeing done, it's time to delve into San Lorenzo's drinking and art scenes. Start at **Said** (☎06 446 92 04; www.said.it; Via Tiburtina 135; praline assortment €8, desserts €8-10; ⏲10am-12.30am Tue-Thu, to 1.30am Fri, noon-1.30am Sat, noon-midnight Sun; 📶; 🚋Reti), a boutique cafe-restaurant set in a 1920s factory. Order a hot chocolate, chocolate martini or other chocolatey temptation.

❹ Esc Atelier

Visit the left-leaning artists and residents who operate this hybrid **arts space and neighbourhood centre** (www.escatelier.net; Via dei Volsci 159; ⏲3-11pm Tue-Sat; 🚋Reti). You're bound to find someone keen to brief you on the local art, literary and political scenes.

❺ Craft Beer

The bar staff at hipster hotspot **Artisan** (☎327 9105709; www.facebook.com/art.isan.90/; Via degli Arunci 9; ⏲6pm-1am Sun & Mon, to 2am Tue-Thu, to 3am Fri & Sat; 🚋Reti) are always happy to recommend particular craft beers from its large range.

❻ Eat with the Beats

The book-lined walls and vintage furnishings at **Officina Beat** (☎06 9521 87 79; https://officinebeat.it; Via degli Equi 29; ⏲6pm-1am Sun-Thu, to 2am Fri & Sat; 📶; 🚋Reti) provide a suitably boho setting for a drink or simple meal.

❼ Nuovo Cinema Palazzo

Fully fuelled, head to this **palace of alternative culture** (www.nuovocinemapalazzo.it; Piazza dei Sanniti 9a; ⏲hours vary; 🚌Via Tiburtina) to experience one of the creative happenings it hosts – film screenings, theatre performances, jazz concerts, breakdance classes.

❽ Last Drinks

Close your day at **Bar Celestino** (☎06 4547 2483; www.facebook.com/bar-celestino; Via degli Ausoni 62-64; ⏲7.30am-2am Mon-Sat; 🚋Reti). Fight your way through the crowd and claim a seat inside or join the grungy regulars drinking on the pavement.

San Giovanni & Celio

Southeast of the centre, the mighty Basilica di San Giovanni in Laterano is the principal drawcard of the handsome, largely residential San Giovanni district. Nearby, the Celio (Caelian), one of Rome's original seven hills, rises to the south of the Colosseum. A tranquil area of medieval churches and graceful greenery, it's ideal for escaping the crowds but offers little after-hours action.

The Short List

- ***Basilica di San Giovanni in Laterano (p134)*** *Facing up to the monumental splendour of what was once Rome's most important church. You'll feel very small as you explore the echoing baroque interior of the city's oldest Christian basilica.*

- ***Basilica di San Clemente (p137)*** *Going underground at this beautiful medieval basilica. Before you exit, check the church's glittering 12th-century apse mosaic.*

- ***Chiesa di Santo Stefano Rotondo (p137)*** *Shivering at the sight of the graphic decor at this haunting ancient church.*

Getting There & Around

Buses 85 and 714 serve San Giovanni from Termini. Bus 87 stops in San Giovanni en route to/from the *centro storico* (historic centre).

M San Giovanni is accessible by metro lines A and C.

Tram 3 runs from San Giovanni to Testaccio and on to Trastevere.

San Giovanni & Celio Map on p136

Chiesa di Santo Stefano Rotondo (p137) STEFANO_VALERI / SHUTTERSTOCK ©

Top Experience

Explore Basilica di San Giovanni in Laterano

This monumental church, the oldest of the city's four papal basilicas, is Rome's official cathedral and the pope's seat as the Bishop of Rome. Dating to the 4th century, it's revered as the mater et caput *(mother and head) of all Catholic churches and was the pope's main place of worship for almost a thousand years.*

MAP P136, E3

06 6988 6493

Piazza di San Giovanni in Laterano 4

basilica free, cloister €5 incl Museo del Tesoro

7am-6.30pm, cloister 9am-6pm

M San Giovanni

The Facade

Crowned by 15 7m-high statues – Christ with St John the Baptist, John the Evangelist and the 12 Apostles – Alessandro Galilei's immense late-baroque facade was added in 1735. In the portico behind the colossal columns, look out for the **central bronze doors** which were moved here from the Curia in the Roman Forum, and, on the far right, the **Holy Door**, which is only opened in Jubilee years.

The Interior

The echoing, marble-clad interior is a breathtaking sight. Designed by Francesco Borromini for the 1650 Jubilee, it features a golden gilt **ceiling**, a 15th-century **mosaic floor**, and a wide **central nave** lined with 18th-century sculptures of the Apostles, each 4.6m high and set in its own dramatic niche.

At the head of the nave, an elaborate Gothic **baldachin** towers over the papal altar. Dating to the 14th century, this is said to contain the relics of the heads of saints Peter and Paul. In front of it, at the base of the altar, the tomb of Pope Martin V lies in the **confessio** along with a wooden statue of St John the Baptist.

The massive **apse** is decorated with sparkling mosaics, some of which survive from the original 4th-century basilica. Most, however, were added in the 1800s.

At the other end of the basilica, you'll find an incomplete **Giotto fresco** on the first pillar in the right-hand nave.

The Cloister

Entered from left of the altar, the basilica's 13th-century cloister is a charming oasis of peace. Set around a central garden, its ambulatories are lined with graceful twisted columns and marble fragments from the original church, including the remains of a 5th-century papal throne and inscriptions of two papal bulls.

★ Top Tips

- Make sure to look down as well as up – the inlaid mosaic floor is a wonderful work of art in its own right.
- In the cloister, look out for a slab of porphyry on which it's said Roman soldiers threw lots to win the robe of the crucified Christ.
- Check out the Giotto fresco on the first column in the right-hand aisle.
- There's an information office to the right of the portico, open 9am to 5pm Monday to Saturday, to 1pm Sunday.

✕ Take a Break

There are few recommended eateries close to the basilica so you'd be better off finishing your tour and heading downhill towards the Colosseum. Here you can lunch on classic trattoria food at Il Bocconcino (p140) or tasty cafe fare at Cafè Cafè (p139).

For reviews see

Top Experiences	p134
Sights	p137
Eating	p139
Drinking	p140
Shopping	p141

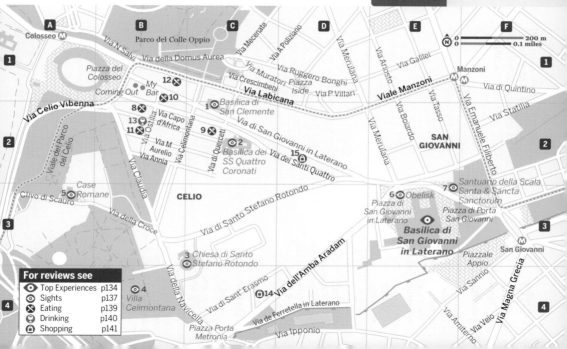

Sights

Basilica di San Clemente

BASILICA

1 MAP P136, C2

Nowhere better illustrates the various stages of Rome's turbulent past than this fascinating multi-layered church. The ground-level 12th-century basilica sits atop a 4th-century church, which, in turn, stands over a 2nd-century pagan temple and a 1st-century Roman house. Beneath everything are foundations dating from the Roman Republic. (06 774 00 21; www.basilicasanclemente.com; Piazza di San Clemente; basilica free, excavations adult/reduced €10/5; 9am-12.30pm & 3-6pm Mon-Sat, 12.15-6pm Sun; Via Labicana)

Basilica dei SS Quattro Coronati

BASILICA

2 MAP P136, C2

This brooding fortified church harbours some lovely 13th-century frescoes and a delightful hidden cloister, accessible from the left-hand aisle. The frescoes, in the **Oratorio di San Silvestro**, depict the story of Constantine and Pope Sylvester I and the so-called Donation of Constantine (p140), a notorious forged document with which the emperor supposedly ceded control of Rome and the Western Roman Empire to the papacy. To access the Oratorio, ring the bell in the second courtyard. (335 495248; Via dei Santi Quattro 20; cloisters €2, Oratorio di San Silvestro €1; basilica 6.30am-12.45pm & 3.30-8pm, cloisters 9.45am-11.45am & 3.45-5.45pm Mon-Sat; Via di San Giovanni in Laterano)

Chiesa di Santo Stefano Rotondo

CHURCH

3 MAP P136, C3

Set in its own secluded grounds, this haunting church boasts a porticoed facade and a round, columned interior. But what really gets the heart racing is the graphic wall decor – a cycle of 16th-century frescoes depicting the tortures suffered by many early Christian martyrs. Describing them in 1846, Charles Dickens wrote: 'Such a panorama of horror and butchery no man could imagine in his sleep, though he were to eat a whole pig, raw, for supper.' (www.santo-stefano-rotondo.it; Via di Santo Stefano Rotondo 7; 10am-1pm & 2-5pm Tue-Sun winter, 10am-1pm & 3.30-6.30pm Tue-Sun summer; Via Claudia)

Villa Celimontana

PARK

4 MAP P136, B4

With its grassy banks and colourful flower beds, this leafy park is a wonderful place to escape the crowds and enjoy a summer picnic. At its centre is a 16th-century villa housing the Italian Geographical Society, while to the south stands a 12m-plus Egyptian obelisk. (Via della Navicella 12; 7am-sunset; Via della Navicella)

Donation of Constantine

The most famous forgery in medieval history, the Donation of Constantine is a document with which Emperor Constantine purportedly grants Pope Sylvester I (r 314–35) and his successors control of Rome and the Western Roman Empire, as well as primacy over the holy sees of Antioch, Alexandria, Constantinople, Jerusalem and all the world's churches.

No one is exactly sure when the document was written, but the consensus is that it dates to the mid- or late 8th century. Certainly this fits with the widespread theory that the author was a Roman cleric, possibly working with the knowledge of Pope Stephen II (r 752–57).

For centuries the donation was accepted as genuine and used by popes to justify their territorial claims. But in 1440 the Italian philosopher Lorenzo Valla proved that it was a forgery. By analysing the Latin used in the document he was able to show that it was inconsistent with the Latin used in the 4th century.

Case Romane

CHRISTIAN SITE

5 MAP P136, A3

According to tradition, two Roman soldiers, John and Paul (not to be confused with the Apostles), lived in these houses before they were beheaded by the emperor Julian. There's no direct evidence for this, although research has revealed that the houses were used for Christian worship. There are more than 20 rooms, many of them richly decorated. (06 7045 4544; www.caseromane.it; Clivo di Scauro; adult/reduced €8/6; 10am-1pm & 3-6pm Thu-Mon; Via Claudia)

Obelisk

MONUMENT

6 MAP P136, E3

Overlooking Palazzo Laterano, this is said to be the world's largest standing Egyptian obelisk. Topping off at almost 46m, it's also the oldest of Rome's 13 ancient obelisks, dating to the 15th century BC. It originally stood in a temple in Thebes but was shipped to Rome by Constantine II and, after various re-locations, placed in its current position in 1588. (Piazza di San Giovanni in Laterano)

Santuario della Scala Santa & Sancta Sanctorum

CHRISTIAN SITE

7 MAP P136, E3

The Scala Santa, said to be the staircase Jesus walked up in Pontius Pilate's palace in Jerusalem, was brought to Rome by St Helena in the 4th century. Pilgrims consider it sacred and climb it on their knees, saying a prayer on each of the 28 steps. At the top, behind an iron grating, is the richly decorated Sancta Sanctorum (Holy of Holies), formerly the pope's private chapel. (www.scala-santa.it; Piazza di San Giovanni in Laterano 14; Scala free, Sancta €3.50; ⌚Scala 6am-2pm & 3-7pm summer, to 6.30pm winter, Sancta Sanctorum 9.30am-12.45pm & 3-4.45pm Mon-Sat; M San Giovanni)

Eating

Cafè Cafè

BISTRO €

8 MAP P136, B2

Cosy, relaxed and welcoming, this cafe-bistro is a far cry from the many impersonal eateries around the Colosseum. With its rustic wooden tables, butternut walls and wine bottles, it's a charming spot for a breakfast pancake, lunch salad or afternoon tea and cake. It will also do you a sandwich and water to go for €5, ideal for a picnic. (☎06 7045 1303; www.cafecafebistrot.it; Via dei Santi Quattro 44; meals €15-20; ⌚9.30am-8.30pm Wed-Mon, to 4pm Tue; 🚌Via di San Giovanni in Laterano)

Li Rioni

PIZZA €

9 MAP P136, C2

Always busy, this boisterous joint serves the best pizza in the Colosseum neighbourhood. Locals and tourists squeeze into the noisy interior – set up as a Roman street scene – and tuck into crispy fried starters and bubbling wood-charred pizzas in the thin-crust Roman style. (☎06 7045 0605; www.lirioni.it; Via dei Santi Quattro

Scala Santa

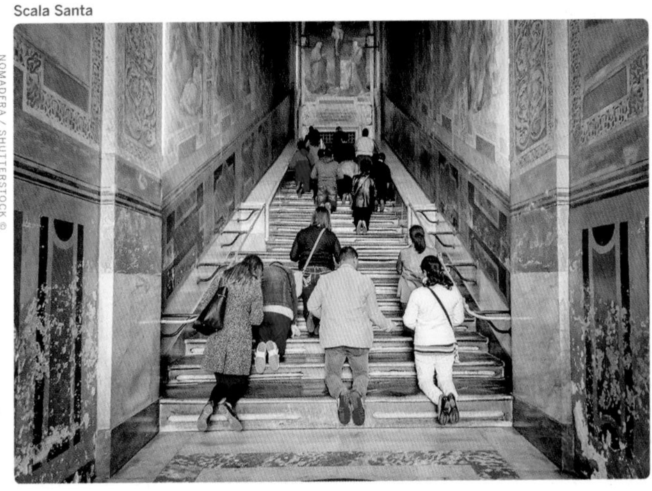

24; meals €15-20; 7pm-midnight Wed-Mon; Via di San Giovanni in Laterano)

Divin Ostilia

ITALIAN €€

10 MAP P136, B1

A popular choice near the Colosseum, Divin Ostilia is a model wine bar with wooden shelves lined with bottles and a high brick ceiling. It's a small place and its cosy interior can get pretty toasty at mealtimes as diners squeeze in to feast on cheese and cured meats, classic pastas and grilled steaks. (06 7049 6526; Via Ostilia 4; meals €30-35; noon-11.30pm, wine bar to 1am; Via Labicana)

Il Bocconcino

LAZIO €€

11 MAP P136, B2

One of the better options in the touristy pocket near the Colosseum, this easy-going trattoria stands out for its authentic regional cooking. Daily specials are chalked up on blackboards or there's a regular menu of classic Roman pastas, grilled meats and imaginative desserts. (06 7707 9175; www.ilbocconcino.com; Via Ostilia 23; meals €30-35; 12.30-3.30pm & 7.30-11.30pm Thu-Tue; Via Labicana)

Aroma

GASTRONOMY €€€

12 MAP P136, B1

One for a special occasion, the rooftop restaurant of the luxury Palazzo Manfredi hotel offers once-in-a-lifetime views of the Colosseum and Michelin-starred food that rises to the occasion. Overseeing the kitchen is chef Giuseppe Di Iorio, whose seasonal menus reflect his passion for creating inventive, forward-thinking Mediterranean cuisine. (06 9761 5109; www.aromarestaurant.it; Via Labicana 125; meals €120-180; 12.30-3pm & 7.30-11.30pm; Via Labicana)

Drinking

Wine Concept

WINE BAR

13 MAP P136, B2

Wine buffs looking to excite their palate should search out this smart *enoteca* (wine bar). Run by expert sommeliers, it has an extensive list of Italian regional labels and European vintages, as well as

Cocktails in a Roman bar

MARCOMERRY / SHUTTERSTOCK ©

a small daily food menu. Wines are available to drink by the glass or buy by the bottle. (06 7720 6673; www.wineconcept.it; Via Capo d'Africa 21; noon-3pm & 6pm-midnight Mon-Thu, noon-3pm & 6pm-1am Fri, 6pm-1am Sat; Via Labicana)

Shopping

Pifebo VINTAGE

14 MAP P136, C4

This is one of Rome's best-stocked secondhand and vintage clothing stores. There is a definite rocker theme to the stock on offer, which includes endless racks of leather jackets, denims, cut-off shorts and cowboy boots. Dig further through the red-painted rooms and you'll discover plenty more to pimp up your wardrobe. (06 9818 5845; https://pifebo.com; Via dei Valeri 10; noon-8pm Mon-Sat; Via dell'Ambra Aradam)

Soul Food MUSIC

15 MAP P136, D2

Run by Hate Records, Soul Food is a laid-back record store with an encyclopaedic collection of vinyl that runs the musical gamut, from '60s garage and rockabilly music to punk, indie, new wave, folk, funk and soul. You will also find retro T-shirts, posters, fanzines, and even vintage toys. (06 7045 2025; www.haterecords.com; Via di San Giovanni in Laterano 192; 10.30am-1.30pm & 3.30-7.30pm Tue-Sat; Via di San Giovanni in Laterano)

Gay Nights

The bottom end of Via di San Giovanni in Laterano, the sloping street that runs from the Basilica di San Giovanni to near the Colosseum, is a favourite haunt of Rome's gay community. In the evenings, bars like **Coming Out** (Map p136, B1; 06 700 98 71; www.comingout.it; Via di San Giovanni in Laterano 8; 7am-5.30am; Via Labicana) and **My Bar** (Map p136, B1; 06 700 44 25; Via di San Giovanni in Laterano 12; 9am-2am; Via Labicana) burst into life, attracting large crowds of mostly gay men.

Aventino & Testaccio

Rising above the mighty ruins of the Terme di Caracalla, the Aventino (Aventine Hill) is a graceful district of elegant villas, lush gardens and austere churches. At the top, Via di Santa Sabina possesses one of Rome's great curiosities – a keyhole view of St Peter's dome. Below, the traditional working-class district of Testaccio is a popular nightlife hang-out and a bastion of classical Roman cuisine.

The Short List

- ***Terme di Caracalla (p147)*** *Being over-awed by the colossal remnants of this vast baths complex. There are better-known ruins in Rome but these rival the best of them.*
- ***Villa del Priorato di Malta (p147)*** *Looking through the unmarked keyhole to enjoy a magical view of St Peter's dome.*
- ***Traditional Trattorias (p144)*** *Enjoying a leisurely meal at one of Testaccio's trattorias is a quintessential Roman experience.*

Getting There & Around

Bus 714 for the Terme di Caracalla.

M For Testaccio take line B to Piramide. The Aventino is walkable from Testaccio and Circo Massimo station (line B).

From San Giovanni tram 3 runs along Viale Aventino, through Testaccio and on to Trastevere.

Aventino & Testaccio Map on p146

Terme di Caracalla (p147) KIEV.VICTOR / SHUTTERSTOCK ©

Walking Tour

A Taste of Testaccio

With its working-class roots and renown as the birthplace of traditional Roman cuisine, Testaccio offers a glimpse of another, less-touristy Rome. It's not completely off the beaten path but it retains a distinct neighbourhood character and its historic market and popular trattorias are much loved locally. Food apart, there's also contemporary art and a grassy hill made of ancient rubbish.

Walk Facts

Start Pasticceria Barberini; metro Piramide

End Barnaba: metro Piramide

Length 2.5km; up to six hours

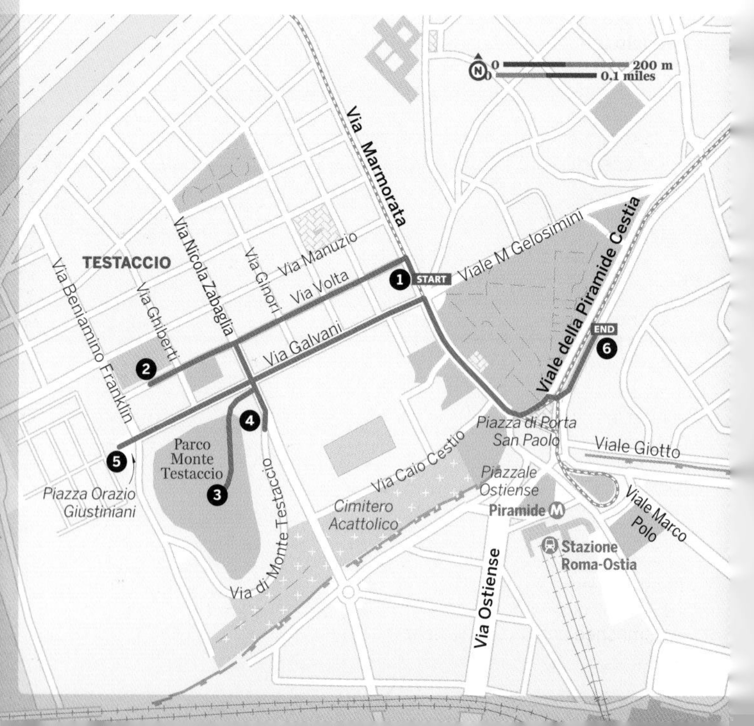

❶ Breakfast at Pasticceria Barberini

Start your day with a bar breakfast at **Pasticceria Barberini** (06 5725 0431; www.pasticceriabarberini.it; Via Marmorata 41; cappuccino & cornetto €2; 6am-9pm; ; M Piramide). To do it Roman-style, stand at the counter and have a *caffè* (or cappuccino) and *cornetto* (a croissant filled with jam or rich chocolate cream).

❷ A Trip to the Market

Testaccio's neighbourhood market, the **Nuovo Mercato di Testaccio** (entrances Via Beniamino Franklin, Via Volta, Via Manuzio, Via Ghiberti; 7am-3.30pm Mon-Sat; Via Marmorata), is as much about people-watching as shopping. Traders cheerfully bellow at one and all until lunchtime when the market's popular food stalls burst into life.

❸ Monte Testaccio

Get to the heart of the local landscape at **Monte Testaccio** (06 06 08; Via Nicolo Zabaglia 24, cnr Via Galvani; adult/reduced €4/3, plus cost of tour; group visits only, reservation necessary; Via Marmorata). This 54m-high grass-capped mound is essentially a huge pile of amphorae fragments (*testae* in Latin), dating to the time when Testaccio was ancient Rome's river port. The amphorae were used to transport wine and oil; once emptied they were smashed and their fragments stacked.

❹ Carbonara at Flavio al Velavevodetto

Sample authentic *cucina romana* (Roman cuisine) at **Flavio al Velavevodetto** (06 574 41 94; www.ristorantevelavevodetto.it; Via di Monte Testaccio 97-99; meals €30-35; 12.30-3pm & 7.45-11pm; Via Galvani). To keep it local, try *carciofo alla giudia* (deep-fried artichoke) followed by superlative *rigatoni alla carbonara* (pasta tubes wrapped in a silky egg sauce spiked with morsels of cured pig's cheek).

❺ Modern Art at the Mattatoio

Spend the afternoon admiring art at the **Mattatoio** (06 3996 7500; www.mattatoioroma.it; Piazza Orazio Giustiniani 4; adult/reduced €6/5; 2-8pm Tue-Sun; Via Marmorata), one of Rome's top contemporary arts venues. The 19th-century complex was the city's main abattoir until 1975 but it now hosts exhibitions and performances by well-known and emerging artists.

❻ Wine at Barnaba

Round the day off with some wine-tasting at **Barnaba** (06 2348 4415; www.facebook.com/barnabawinebarecucina; Via della Piramide Cestia 45-51; meal €38; 12.30pm-12.30am; ; M Piramide), a fashionable wine bar with a strong selection of natural and independent Italian labels as well as champagnes and wines by the glass.

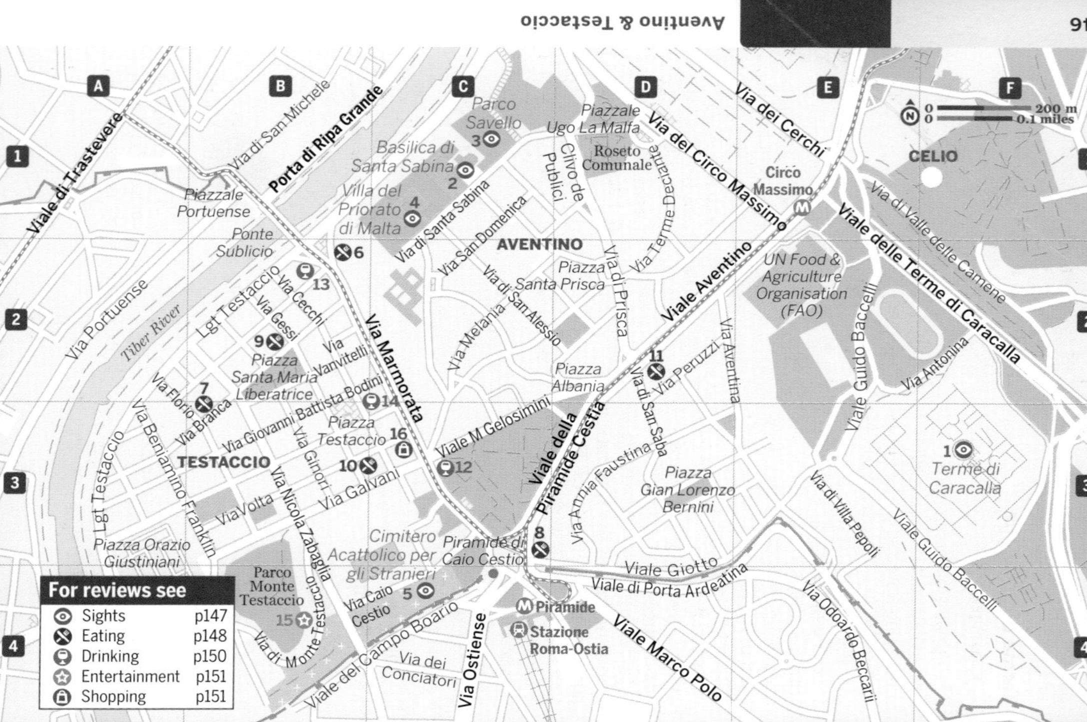
A
B
C
D
E
F
1
2
3
4
200 m
0.1 miles
CELIO
AVENTINO
TESTACCIO
Viale di Trastevere
Via di San Michele
Porta di Ripa Grande
Piazzale Portuense
Ponte Sublicio
Via Portuense
Tiber River
Lgt Testaccio
Via Cecchi
Via Gessi
Via Vanvitelli
Piazza Santa Maria Liberatrice
Via Florio
Via Branca
Via Giovanni Battista Bodini
Piazza Testaccio
Via Ginori
Via Galvani
Via Beniamino Franklin
Via Volta
Via Nicola Zabaglia
Piazza Orazio Giustiniani
Parco Monte Testaccio
Via di Monte Testaccio
Via Caio Cestio
Viale del Campo Boario
Via dei Conciatori
Via Ostiense
Cimitero Acattolico per gli Stranieri
Piramide di Caio Cestio
Piramide
Stazione Roma-Ostia
Viale Marco Polo
Via Marmorata
Parco Savello
Basilica di Santa Sabina
Villa del Priorato di Malta
Via di Santa Sabina
Via San Domenica
Via Melania
Via di San Alessio
Piazza Santa Prisca
Via di Prisca
Piazzale Ugo La Malfa
Clivo de Publici
Roseto Comunale
Via Terme Deciante
Via del Circo Massimo
Via dei Cerchi
Circo Massimo
Viale Aventino
Piazza Albania
Viale M Gelosimini
Viale della Piramide Cestia
Via di San Saba
Via Peruzzi
Via Aventina
Via Annia Faustina
Piazza Gian Lorenzo Bernini
Viale Giotto
Viale di Porta Ardeatina
Via Odoardo Beccari
Via di Villa Pepoli
Viale Guido Baccelli
UN Food & Agriculture Organisation (FAO)
Via Antonina
Viale delle Terme di Caracalla
Via di Valle delle Camene
Terme di Caracalla
1
2
3
4
5
6
7
8
9
10
11
12
13
14
15
16
For reviews see
Sights p147
Eating p148
Drinking p150
Entertainment p151
Shopping p151

Sights

Terme di Caracalla

RUINS

1 MAP P146, F3

The remains of the emperor Caracalla's vast baths complex are among Rome's most awe-inspiring ruins. Inaugurated in AD 216, the original 10-hectare site, which comprised baths, gyms, libraries, shops and gardens, was used by up to 8000 people daily. Most of the ruins are what's left of the central bathhouse. This was a huge rectangular edifice book-ended by two **palestre** (gyms) and centred on a **frigidarium** (cold room), where bathers would stop after the warmer **tepidarium** and dome-capped **caldarium** (hot room). (06 3996 7700; www.coopculture.it; Viale delle Terme di Caracalla 52; adult/reduced €8/4; 9am-1hr before sunset Tue-Sun, 9am-2pm Mon; Viale delle Terme di Caracalla)

Basilica di Santa Sabina

BASILICA

2 MAP P146, C1

This solemn basilica, one of Rome's most beautiful early Christian churches, was founded by Peter of Illyria around AD 422. It was enlarged in the 9th century and again in 1216, just before it was given to the newly founded Dominican order – note the tombstone of Muñoz de Zamora, one of the order's founding fathers, in the nave floor. The interior was further modified by Domenico Fontana in 1587. A 20th-century restoration subsequently returned it to its original look. (06 57 94 01; Piazza Pietro d'Illiria 1; 6.30am-12.45pm & 3-8pm; Lungotevere Aventino)

Parco Savello

PARK

3 MAP P146, C1

Known to Romans as the *Giardino degli Aranci* (Orange Garden), this walled park is a romantic haven. Head down the central avenue, passing towering umbrella pines and lawns planted with blooming orange trees, to bask in heavenly sunset views of St Peter's dome and the city's rooftops. (Via di Santa Sabina; 7am-9pm summer, to 6pm winter; Via del Circo Massimo)

Villa del Priorato di Malta

HISTORIC BUILDING

4 MAP P146, C1

Fronting an ornate cypress-shaded piazza, the Roman headquarters of the Sovereign Order of Malta, aka the *Cavalieri di Malta* (Knights of Malta), boasts one of Rome's most celebrated views. It's not immediately apparent, but look through the keyhole in the villa's green door and you'll see the dome of St Peter's Basilica perfectly aligned at the end of a hedge-lined avenue. (Villa Magistrale; Piazza dei Cavalieri di Malta; Lungotevere Aventino)

All About Offal

The hallmark of an authentic Roman menu is the presence of offal. The Roman love of nose-to-tail eating arose in Testaccio around the city abattoir, and many of its neighbourhood trattorias serve traditional offal-based dishes. So whether you want to avoid them or give them a go, look out for *pajata* (veal intestines), *trippa* (tripe), *coda alla vaccinara* (oxtail), *coratella* (heart, lung and liver), *animelle* (sweetbreads), *testarella* (head), *lingua* (tongue) and *zampe* (trotters).

Cimitero Acattolico per gli Stranieri

CEMETERY

5 MAP P146, C4

Despite the roads that surround it, Rome's 'non-Catholic' cemetery is a verdant oasis of peace. An air of Grand Tour romance hangs over the site where up to 4000 people are buried, including poets Keats and Shelley, and Italian political thinker Antonio Gramsci. Among the gravestones and cypress trees, look out for the *Angelo del Dolore (Angel of Grief)*, a much-replicated 1894 sculpture that US artist William Wetmore Story created for his wife's grave. (06 574 19 00; www.cemeteryrome.it; Via Caio Cestio 6; voluntary donation €3; 9am-5pm Mon-Sat, to 1pm Sun; M Piramide)

Eating

Giulietta

PIZZA €

6 MAP P146, B2

Occupying a former car showroom, this trendy pizzeria is part of a multi-space food hub part-owned by top Roman chef Cristina Bowerman. Its cavernous dining area, decorated in abstract contemporary style, sets the stage for sensational wood-fired pizzas topped with prime Italian ingredients. (06 4522 9022; https://giuliettapizzeria.it; Piazza dell'Emporio 28; pizzas €6.50-13; 7.30pm-11.30pm; Via Marmorata)

Trapizzino

FAST FOOD €

7 MAP P146, B3

The original of what is now a growing countrywide chain, this is the birthplace of the *trapizzino*, a kind of hybrid sandwich made by stuffing a cone of doughy focaccia with fillers like *polpette al sugo* (meatballs in tomato sauce) or *pollo alla cacciatore* (stewed chicken). They're messy to eat but quite delicious. (06 4341 9624; www.trapizzino.it; Via Branca 88; trapizzini from €3.50; noon-1am Tue-Sun; Via Marmorata)

Paraponzipò

SANDWICHES €

8 MAP P146, C3

Paraponzipò proves that the best thing since sliced bread is superb Italian salumi and cheese packed between said bread. An impressive selection of cold cuts such as mortadella, porchetta and bresaola stands alongside piled-high fish and vegetarian options – everything from sun-dried tomatoes to *pecorino* to truffle cream. Seating is sparse – grab your *panino* to go. (☎06 4542 8690; www.paraponzipo.it; Piazza di Porta San Paolo 9; sandwiches €5-6; ⏲10.30am-10pm Thu-Sat, to 5pm Tue, Wed & Sun, to 4pm Mon; ; Ⓜ Piramide)

Pizzeria Da Remo PIZZA €

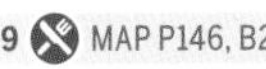
9 MAP P146, B2

For an authentic Roman experience, join the noisy crowds here at one of the city's best-known and most popular pizzerias. It's a spartan-looking place, but the crispy wafer-thin pizzas, served charred and spilling over the plate's edges, are the business, and there's a cheerful, boisterous vibe. Expect to queue after 8.30pm. (☎06 574 62 70; Piazza Santa Maria Liberatrice 44; meals €15; ⏲7pm-1am Mon-Sat; 🚌Via Marmorata)

Da Felice ROMAN €€

10 MAP P146, B3

This historic trattoria, much frequented by locals and tourists alike, is renowned for its unswerving dedication to Roman soul food. In contrast to the light-touch modern decor, the menu is pure old school with hallowed city staples such as *tonnarelli a cacio e pepe* (thick spaghetti with *pecorino* cheese and ground black pepper). Reservations essential. (☎06 574 68 00; www.feliceatestaccio.it; Via Mastro Giorgio 29; meals €30-40; ⏲12.30-3pm & 7-11.30pm; 🚌Via Marmorata)

Trippa (tripe)

Marco Martini Restaurant

GASTRONOMY €€€

11 MAP P146, D2

A lush garden pavilion at the **Corner Townhouse** (06 4554 8810; https://thecornerrome.com; Viale Aventino 121; d €161-301, ste €200-391; ; Viale Aventino, Viale Aventino) provides the lovely setting for this casual fine-dining restaurant. The man with his name on the menu is one of Rome's youngest Michelin-starred chefs, whose inventive dishes often riff on Italian culinary traditions. Order à la carte or opt for one of several tasting menus, including one for vegetarians. (06 4559 7350; http://marcomartinichef.com; Viale Aventino 121; meals from €65, tasting menus from €100; 12.30-2.30pm & 7-10pm, closed Sat lunch & Sun; ; Viale Aventino, Viale Aventino)

Drinking

Tram Depot

BAR

12 MAP P146, C3

When temperatures climb in the capital this charming little bar springs to life, serving up coffee and cocktails (€5) until long after sunset. Its outdoor seating, vintage porch swings, twinkly tea lights and a verdant stretch of grass flanked by trees conjure up a garden-party vibe smack in the centre of the city. (www.facebook.com/tramdepotroma; Via Marmorata 13; 7.30am-2am Mon-Fri, from 9am Sat & Sun May-Oct; M Piramide)

Cheese on display at Volpetti

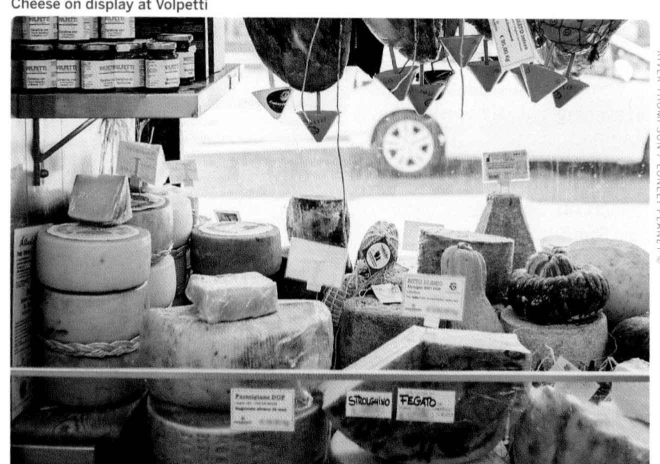

RIVER THOMPSON / LONELY PLANET ©

Rec 23

BAR

13 MAP P146, B2

All exposed brick and mismatched furniture, this large, New York–inspired venue caters to all moods, serving *aperitivo* (drink plus buffet €10), restaurant meals and a weekend brunch (€18). Arrive thirsty to take on a 'Testaccio mule', one of its original cocktails, or keep it simple with an Italian prosecco, Scottish whisky or Latin American rum. (06 8746 2147; www.rec23.com; Piazza dell'Emporio 2; 6.30pm-2am daily, plus 12.30-3.30pm Sat & Sun; Via Marmorata)

L'Oasi della Birra

BAR

14 MAP P146, C2

Housed in the Palombi Enoteca bottle shop, L'Oasi della Birra is exactly that – an oasis of beer. With hundreds of labels, from German heavyweights to British bitters and Belgian brews, plus wines, cheeses and cold cuts, it's ideally set up for an evening's quaffing, either in the cramped cellar or on the piazza-side terrace. Good *aperitivo* buffet too (€10). (06 574 61 22; Piazza Testaccio 41; 4.30pm-1am Mon-Sat, from 6pm Sun; Via Marmorata)

Entertainment

ConteStaccio

LIVE MUSIC

15 MAP P146, B4

A fixture on Rome's music scene, ConteStaccio is one of the top venues on the Testaccio clubbing strip. It's known for its free gigs which feature both emerging groups and established performers, spanning a range of styles – indie, pop, rock, acoustic, reggae, new wave. Also serves food. (www.facebook.com/contestaccio; Via di Monte Testaccio 65b; 6pm-5am Wed-Sat; Via Galvani)

Al Fresco Opera

The hulking ruins of the vast 3rd-century Terme di Caracalla (p147) set the memorable stage for the summer season of music and ballet from **Teatro dell'Opera** (www.operaroma.it; Viale delle Terme di Caracalla 52; tickets from €30; Jun & Jul; Viale delle Terme di Caracalla), with performances by big-name Italian and international artists.

Shopping

Volpetti

FOOD & DRINKS

16 MAP P146, C3

This super-stocked deli, one of the best in town, is a treasure trove of gourmet delicacies. Helpful staff will guide you through its extensive selection of Italian cheeses, homemade pastas, olive oils, vinegars, cured meats, wines and grappas. It also serves excellent, though pricey, sliced pizza. (06 574 23 52; www.volpetti.com; Via Marmorata 47; 8.30am-2pm & 4.30-8.15pm Mon-Fri, 8.30am-8.30pm Sat; Via Marmorata)

Walking Tour

Ostiense & San Paolo

Packed with post-industrial grit, Ostiense is all about exuberant street art, cutting-edge clubs and cool bars. The presence of a university campus lends a buzz, and its disused factories provide space for all sorts of after-hours hedonism. Traditional sights are thin on the ground, but you'll find a fabulous post-industrial art museum and the world's third-largest church.

Getting There

Ostiense extends south of the city centre along Via Ostiense.

M Line B runs to Piramide, Garbatella and Basilica San Paolo.

Routes 23 and 769 serve Via Ostiense.

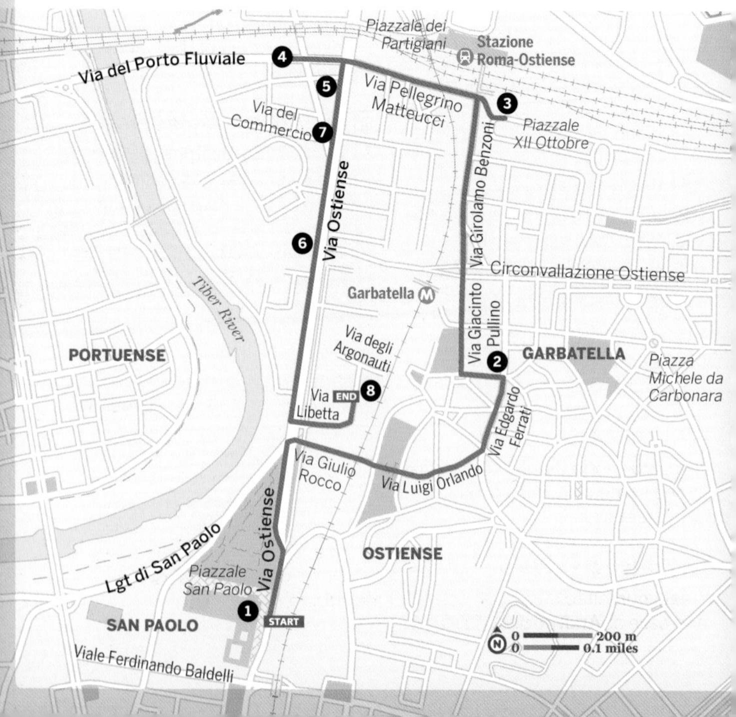

❶ Basilica di San Paolo Fuori le Mura

Start your tour at the vast **Basilica di San Paolo Fuori le Mura** (Basilica of St Paul Outside the Walls; ☎06 6988 0803; www.basilicasanpaolo.org; Piazzale San Paolo 1; cloisters adult/reduced €4/3; ⏰7am-6.30pm; Ⓜ Basilica San Paolo). Much of the original basilica was destroyed by fire in 1823, but some features survived, including the 5th-century triumphal arch and Gothic tabernacle.

❷ Garbatella

To experience one of Rome's most idiosyncratic neighbourhoods, make for Garbatella, a colourful garden suburb developed in the 1920s and '30s.

❸ Lunch at Eataly

For lunch, push on to **Eataly** (☎06 9027 9201; www.eataly.net; Piazzale XII Ottobre 1492; meals €10-50; ⏰shops 9am-midnight, restaurants typically noon-3.30pm & 7-11pm; 📶; Ⓜ Piramide, 🚆 Ostiense), a vast foodie complex with nearly 20 restaurants and cafes.

❹ Street Art

Stroll down **Via del Porto Fluviale** to see some of Rome's most inventive street murals.

❺ Coffee & Cakes

Treat yourself to afternoon coffee and cake at **Andreotti** (☎06 575 07 73; www.andreottiroma.it; Via Ostiense 54; treats from €1.50; ⏰7.30am-10pm; 📶; 🚌 Via Ostiense, Ⓜ Piramide), a favourite of local film director Ferzan Ozpetek.

❻ Centrale Montemartini

In an ex-powerplant ancient sculpture is juxtaposed against engines and furnaces at the **Centrale Montemartini** (Museums at Centrale Montemartini; ☎06 06 08; www.centralemontemartini.org; off Via Ostiense 106; adult/reduced €7.50/6.50, incl Capitoline Museums €12.50/10.50, ticket valid 7 days; ⏰9am-7pm Tue-Sun; 🚌 Via Ostiense), a striking outpost of the Capitoline Museums.

❼ Aperitivo at Doppiozeroo

Between 6pm and 9pm, urbane Romans flock to **Doppiozeroo** (☎06 5730 1961; www.doppiozeroo.com; Via Ostiense 68; meals €12-35; ⏰7am-2am; 🚌 Via Ostiense, Ⓜ Piramide) for its lavish *aperitivo* buffet selection.

❽ Cool Clubbing

While the clubs get going late, you can start off at **Azienda Cucineria** (☎327 7615286; www.circolodegliilluminati.it; Via Giuseppe Libetta 3; ⏰kitchen 8pm-midnight Tue-Sat, club 10.30pm-late Thu-Sat; Ⓜ Garbatella), which serves food in a romantic outdoor setting before morphing into the club, **Circolo Degli Illuminati**.

Catacombe di San Callisto

Worth a Trip

Traverse the Via Appia Antica

The Appian Way was known to the Romans as Regina Viarum (Queen of Roads). Named after Appius Claudius Caecus, who laid the first 90km section in 312 BC, it was extended in 190 BC to reach Brindisi on the Adriatic coast. Today it's one of Rome's most exclusive addresses, a beautiful cobbled thoroughfare flanked by fields, Roman ruins and towering pines.

Appian Way

06 513 53 16

www.parcoappiaantica.it

main site 24hr, individual sites hours vary

Via Appia Antica

Catacombe di San Callisto

The most-visited **catacombs** (☎06 513 01 51; www.catacombe.roma.it; Via Appia Antica 110-126; adult/reduced €8/5; ⏱9am-noon & 2-5pm Thu-Tue Mar-Jan) in Rome, these extend for more than 20km in a tangle of tunnels. Visits are only by tour, and you'll visit just a fraction of what lies below ground. Still, you'll see a selection of tombs that includes 16 popes, scores of martyrs and thousands upon thousands of Christians.

Catacombe di Santa Domitilla

Well away from the main swath of Via Appia Antica sights, these **catacombs** (☎06 511 03 42; www.domitilla.info; Via delle Sette Chiese 282; adult/reduced €8/5; ⏱9am-noon & 2-5pm Wed-Mon mid-Jan–mid-Dec) feature the evocative underground **Chiesa di SS Nereus e Achilleus**, a 4th-century church dedicated to two Roman soldiers martyred by Diocletian.

On a tour, you'll see the church, some exquisite Christian wall art and just a fraction of the tunnels, which extend roughly 17km. The site is below what was the private burial ground of Flavia Domitilla, niece of the emperor Domitian and a member of the wealthy Flavian family.

Basilica & Catacombe di San Sebastiano

One of the two main Appian Way catacombs, this complex contains frescoes, stucco work, epigraphs and immaculately preserved mausoleums. The catacombs extend for more than 12km and once harboured more than 65,000 tombs.

The original 4th-century **basilica** (☎06 780 88 47; www.sansebastianofuorilemura.org; Via Appia Antica 136; ⏱8.30am-6.30pm) was mostly destroyed in the 9th century and the church you see today dates mainly from the 17th century. It is dedicated to St Sebastian, who was martyred and buried here in the late 3rd century. In the

★ Top Tips

- Bikes are available to rent at **Appia Antica Caffè** (☎06 8987 9575; www.appiaanticacaffe.it; Via Appia Antica 175; per hr/day €4/15; ⏱9am-sunset Tue-Sun, to 2pm Mon; 🚌Via di Cecilia Metella). Don't cycle north of the cafe due to busy roads, steep hills and uneven pavements.
- Visits to the catacombs are by guided tour only. Wear sensible shoes and dress warmly.

✕ Take a Break

Enjoy a garden lunch at **Il Giardino di Giulia e Fratelli** (☎347 5092772; Via Appia Antica 176; meals €10-30; ⏱noon-3pm & 7-11.30pm Tue-Sat; 👪; 🚌Via Appia Antica), near the Mausoleo di Cecilia Metella.

★ Getting There

Metro & Bus Take line B to Circo Massimo, then bus No 118. Or line A to Colli-Albani, then bus 660.

Capella delle Reliquie you'll find one of the arrows used to kill him and the column to which he was tied.

A warren of tunnels that lie beneath the church, the **Catacombe di San Sebastiano** (☎06 785 03 50; www.catacombe.org; Via Appia Antica 136; adult/reduced €8/5; ⏰10am-5pm Mon-Sat Jan-Nov) were the first catacombs to be so called, the name deriving from the Greek *kata* (near) and *kymbas* (cavity), because they were located near a cave. During the persecution of Christians by the emperor Vespasian from AD 258, some believe that the catacombs were used as a safe haven for the remains of St Peter and St Paul.

Villa di Massenzio

Maxentius' huge 4th-century palace complex features the **Circo di Massenzio** (☎06 06 08; www.villadimassenzio.it; Via Appia Antica 153; admission free; ⏰10am-4pm Tue-Sun), Rome's best-preserved ancient racetrack – you can still make out the starting stalls used for chariot races. The 10,000-seat arena was built by Maxentius around 309, but he died before ever seeing a race here.

Overlooking the vast site, the namesake **Villa di Massenzio** (☎06 06 08; www.villadimassenzio.it; Via Appia Antica 153; admission free; ⏰10am-4pm Tue-Sun) itself is closed for long-term archaeological investigations.

Mausoleo di Cecilia Metella

Resembling a huge can of tomatoes, this **mausoleum** (☎06 3996 7700; www.coopculture.it; Via Appia Antica 161; adult/reduced €5/2.50, incl Villa dei Quintili & Complesso di Santa Maria Nova €10; ⏰9am-1pm & 2-5pm Mon-Fri, 9am-2pm Sat) from the 1st century BC encloses a now roofless burial chamber. In the 14th century it was converted into a fort by the Caetani family and used to collect tolls from passing traffic.

Villa dei Quintili

This 2nd-century **villa** (☎06 3996 7700; www.coopculture.it; main entrance: Via Appia Antica 251, east entrance: Via Appia Nuova 1092; adult/reduced incl Mausoleo di Cecilia Metella valid for 2 days €5/2.50; ⏰9am-1hr before sunset Tue-Sun; 🚌Via Appia Nuova) is one of Rome's least-visited major sights. It was the lavish home of two consuls, the Quintili brothers, but its luxurious excess was their downfall: the emperor Commodus had them both killed and seized the villa for himself. The emperor expanded the complex and the remaining ruins retain their opulence. Don't miss the baths complex with a pool, *caldarium* (hot bath room) and *frigidarium* (cold bath room) and the small museum, which offers useful context.

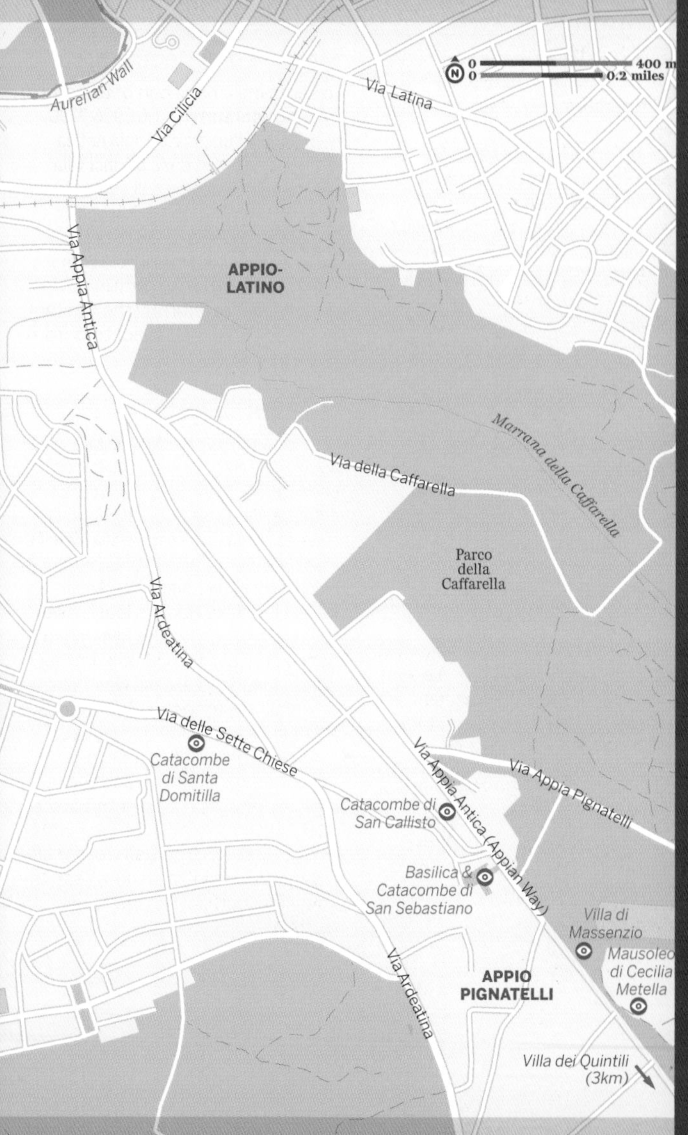
0 400 m
0 0.2 miles
Aurelian Wall
Via Cilicia
Via Latina
Via Appia Antica
APPIO-
LATINO
Marrana della Caffarella
Via della Caffarella
Parco
della
Caffarella
Via Ardeatina
Via delle Sette Chiese
Catacombe
di Santa
Domitilla
Via Appia Antica (Appian Way)
Via Appia Pignatelli
Catacombe di
San Callisto
Basilica &
Catacombe di
San Sebastiano
Villa di
Massenzio
Mausoleo
di Cecilia
Metella
Via Ardeatina
APPIO
PIGNATELLI
Villa dei Quintili
(3km)

Trastevere & Gianicolo

With its old-world cobbled lanes, ochre palazzi, ivy-clad facades and boho vibe, ever-trendy Trastevere is one of Rome's most vivacious neighbourhoods. Endlessly photogenic, its labyrinth of backstreet lanes heaves after dark as crowds swarm to its foodie and fashionable restaurants, cafes and bars. Rising up behind all this, Gianicolo Hill offers superb views.

The Short List

- ***Basilica di Santa Maria in Trastevere (p160)*** *Admiring exquisite mosaics in this beautiful church, followed by people-watching on the square in front.*
- ***Trattoria dining (p168)*** *Feasting on Roman food at traditional trattorias on tiny cobbled piazzas.*
- ***Villa Farnesina (p165)*** *Savouring Raphael's breathtaking decor at this elegant Renaissance villa.*
- ***Nightlife (p169)*** *Sampling inventive cocktails, trying fine wines and hobnobbing with hipsters in secret speakeasies.*
- ***Gianicolo (p166)*** *Hiking to the top of Rome's highest hill for soul-soaring panoramas.*

Getting There & Around

Tram 8 from Largo di Torre Argentina. Tram 3 for the southern end of Viale Trastevere, connecting with Testaccio, Colosseo, San Giovanni, Villa Borghese.

Bus H from Termini; bus 780 from Piazza Venezia. For Gianicolo, bus 870 from Piazza della Rovere, bus 115 from Viale di Trastevere.

Trastevere & Giancolo Map on p164

Piazza di Santa Maria in Trastevere (p163) CATARINA BELOVA / SHUTTERSTOCK ©

Top Experience

Visit Basilica di Santa Maria in Trastevere

This glittering church is said to be the oldest church in Rome dedicated to the Virgin Mary. It was first constructed in the early 3rd century over the spot where, according to legend, a fountain of oil miraculously sprang from the ground. Its current Romanesque form is the result of a 12th-century revamp.

MAP P164, B3

06 581 48 02

Piazza Santa Maria in Trastevere

7.30am-9pm Sep-Jul, 8am-noon & 4-9pm Aug

Viale di Trastevere, Belli

Facade

The church facade is decorated with a beautiful medieval mosaic depicting Mary feeding Jesus surrounded by 10 women bearing lamps. Two are veiled and hold extinguished lamps, symbolising widowhood, while the lit lamps of the others represent their virginity. The portico was added by Carlo Fontana in 1702, its balustrade decorated with statues of four popes.

Mosaics

Inside, it's the golden 12th-century mosaics that stand out. In the apse, look out for the dazzling depiction of Christ and his mother flanked by various saints and, on the far left, Pope Innocent II holding a model of the church. Beneath this is a series of six mosaics by Pietro Cavallini (c 1291) illustrating the life of the Virgin.

Interior Design

Note the 24 Roman columns, some plundered from the Terme di Caracalla; the fragments of Roman carved marbles forming an informal mosaic on the porch; the wooden ceiling designed in 1617 by Domenichino; and, on the right of the altar, a spiralling Cosmati candlestick, on the exact spot where the oil fountain is said to have sprung. The Cappella Avila is also worth a look for its stunning 17th-century dome. The spiralling Cosmatesque floor was relaid in the 1870s, a re-creation of the 13th-century original.

★ Top Tips

- Allow plenty of time to linger on the piazza in front of the church afterwards – it's Trastevere's focal square and a prime people-watching spot.
- Visit early in the morning or at the end of the day when the softer light shows off the beautiful Romanesque facade fresh from a painstaking restoration.

Take a Break

Grab a cappuccino or a glass of Rome's cheapest beer at Bar San Calisto (p169), a local haunt just footsteps from the touristy church square.

Get a slice of some of Trastevere's best pizza at La Renella (p167); the available varieties change by the minute.

Walking Tour

A Night Out in Trastevere & Gianicolo

With its enchanting lanes, vibrant piazzas and carnival atmosphere, Trastevere is one of the city's favourite after-dark hang-outs. Foreigners love it, but it's also a local haunt and Romans come here in droves, particularly on balmy summer nights when street sellers set up camp on the picturesque alleyways and bar crowds spill out onto the streets.

Walk Facts

Start Piazzale Giuseppe Garibaldi; bus 115, 870

End Niji Roma; bus Belli

Length 2.8km; four hours

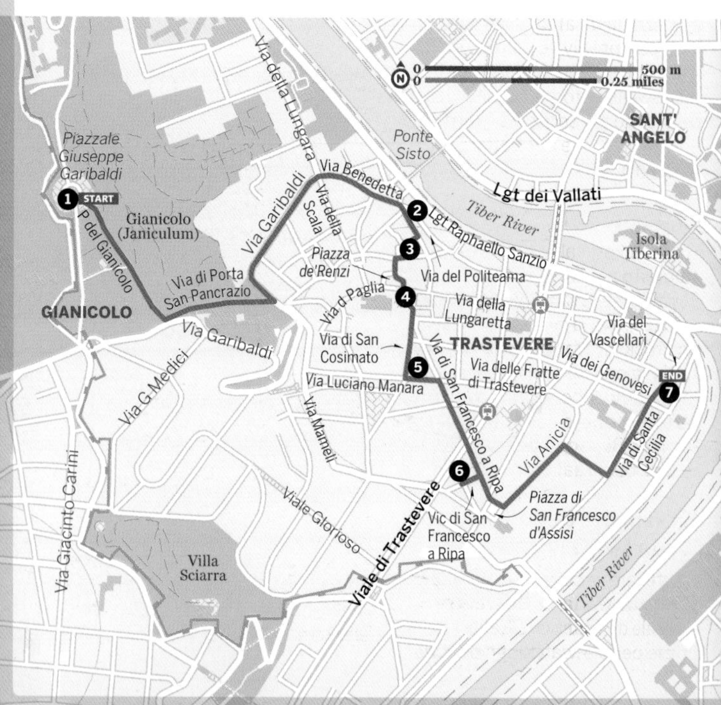

❶ Views on the Gianicolo

The early evening is a good time to enjoy sweeping panoramic views from the **Gianicolo** (p166). This leafy hill, Rome's highest, was the scene of vicious fighting during Italian unification but is now a tranquil, romantic spot.

❷ Aperitivo at Freni e Frizioni

Once back down in the fray, head to **Freni e Frizioni** (06 4549 7499; www.freniefrizioni.com; Via del Politeama 4-6; 6.30pm-2am; Piazza Trilussa) for an *aperitivo*. This perennially cool bar pulls in a spritz-loving young crowd that swells onto the small piazza outside to sip cocktails (from €10) and fill up at the bar buffet (7pm to 10pm).

❸ Dinner at Da Augusto

Bag a rickety table outside **Da Augusto** (06 580 37 98; Piazza de' Renzi 15; meals €25-35; 12.30-3pm & 8-11pm; Via della Scala, Belli) and tuck into fabulous family-style cooking on one of Trastevere's most atmospheric piazza terraces. All the Roman classics are dished up here. Be prepared to queue and expect basic bathrooms.

❹ Hanging Out on Piazza di Santa Maria in Trastevere

Trastevere's main square, **Piazza di Santa Maria in Trastevere** (Viale di Trastevere, Belli), is prime people-watching territory. By day it's full of cheery locals and guidebook-toting tourists; by night foreign students, marauding Romans and hijinks-minded visitors take over.

❺ A Sweet Pause at Otaleg

Let the precious flavours of Marco Radicioni tickle your tastebuds at **Otaleg** (338 6515450; www.otaleg.com; Via di San Cosimato 14a; gelato from €2; noon-midnight; ; Trastevere/Mastai) (gelato spelled backwards). Try the pistachio, lemon and dark chocolate or seasonal surprises like prickly pear and acacia honey.

❻ Blues at Big Mama

To wallow in the Eternal City blues, there's only one place to go – **Big Mama** (06 581 25 51; www.bigmama.it; Vicolo di San Francesco a Ripa 18; 9pm-1.30am, shows 10.30pm, closed summer; Viale di Trastevere, Trastevere/Mastai), a cramped Trastevere basement. There are weekly residencies and frequent blues, jazz, funk, soul and R&B concerts.

❼ Cocktails at Niji Roma

Finish your night late at **Niji Roma** (06 581 95 20; www.facebook.com/niji.cafe.roma; Via dei Vascellari 35; 7pm-3am; Belli), a chic and arty bar with a surreal vibe. Cocktails are exquisitely presented and almost too pretty to drink. The mellow atmosphere is the perfect end to a fine night.

A B C D
1 2 3 4 5 6

CENTRO STORICO
REGOLA
SANT' ANGELO
TRASTEVERE
0 200 m
0 0.1 miles
Lgt della Farnesina
Lgt dei Tebaldi
Via Giulia
Via del Monserrato
Via dei Giubbonari
Via della Lungara
Via dei Riari
Tiber River
Via dei Pettinari
Via Arenula
Via delle Zoccolette
Ponte Sisto
Piazza Trilussa
Lgt dei Vallati
Lgt de Cenci
Via Benedetta
Via del Politeama
Lgt Raphaello Sanzio
Ponte Garibaldi
Isola Tiberina
Ponte Cestio
Via Garibaldi
Via del Mattonato
Via della Scala
Vic del Cinque
Via del Moro
Piazza Sant'Egidio
Via Renella
Via della Lungaretta
Piazza Belli
Piazza Sonnino
Sora Mirella Caffè
Piazza in Piscinula
Via dei Salumi
Via della Luce
Via dei Vascellari
Via di Santa Cecilia
Via Luciano Manara
Piazza San Cosimato
Via di San Francesco a Ripa
Piazza Mastai
Via Mameli
Via Sacchi
Via Morosini
Viale di Trastevere
Via Anicia
Via di San Michele
Piazza di San Francesco d'Assisi
Porta di Ripa Grande
Lgt Aventino
Via F Casini
Viale Glorioso
Piazza Porta Portese
Mercado de Porta Portese
Ponte Sublicio
Via Portuense
Piazza dell'Emporio
Via Marmorata
Lgt Testaccio
Gianicolo (Janiculum)

Basilica di Santa Maria in Trastevere
1 Basilica di Santa Cecilia in Trastevere
2 Villa Farnesina
3 Galleria Corsini
4 Orto Botanico
3 Tempietto di Bramante & Chiesa di San Pietro in Montorio
5
6 Gianicolo
4 18 Via Garibaldi
7
8
9
10
11
12
13
14
15
16
17
19
20
21
22
23

For reviews see

Top Experiences	p160
Sights	p165
Eating	p167
Drinking	p169
Entertainment	p170
Shopping	p170

Sights

Basilica di Santa Cecilia in Trastevere BASILICA

1 MAP P164, D4

The last resting place of the patron saint of music features Pietro Cavallini's stunning 13th-century fresco, in the nuns' choir of the hushed convent adjoining the church. Inside the church itself, Stefano Maderno's mysterious sculpture depicts St Cecilia's miraculously preserved body, unearthed in the Catacombs of San Callisto in 1599. You can also visit the excavations of Roman houses, one of which was possibly Cecilia's. The church is fronted by a gentle fountain surrounded by roses. (06 4549 2739; www.benedettinesantacecilia.it; Piazza di Santa Cecilia 22; fresco & crypt each €2.50; basilica & crypt 10am-12.30pm & 4-6pm Mon-Sat, 11.30am-12.30pm & 4.30-6.30pm Sun, fresco 10am-12.30pm Mon-Sat, 11.30am-12.30pm Sun; Viale de Trastevere, Belli)

Villa Farnesina HISTORIC BUILDING

2 MAP P164, A2

The interior of this gorgeous 16th-century villa is fantastically frescoed from top to bottom. Several paintings in the **Loggia of Cupid and Psyche** and the **Loggia of Galatea**, both on the ground floor, are attributed to Raphael. On the 1st floor, Peruzzi's dazzling frescoes in the **Salone delle Prospettive** are a superb illusionary perspective of a colonnade and panorama of 16th-century Rome. (06 6802 7268; www.villafarnesina.it; Via della Lungara 230; adult/reduced €6/5; 9am-2pm Mon-Sat, to 5pm 2nd Sun of the month; Lungotevere della Farnesina)

Galleria Corsini GALLERY

3 MAP P164, A2

Once home to Queen Christina of Sweden, whose bedroom witnessed a steady stream of male and female lovers, the 16th-century Palazzo Corsini was designed by Ferdinando Fuga in grand Versailles style, and houses part of Italy's national art collection. Highlights include Caravaggio's *San Giovanni Battista* (St John the Baptist), Guido Reni's *Salome con la Testa di San Giovanni Battista* (Salome with the Head of John the Baptist), and Fra' Angelico's Corsini Triptych, plus works by Rubens, Poussin and Van Dyck. (Palazzo Corsini; 06 6880 2323; www.barberinicorsini.org; Via della Lungara 10; adult/reduced incl Palazzo Barberini €12/6; 8.30am-7pm Wed-Mon; Lungotevere della Farnesina)

Orto Botanico GARDENS

4 MAP P164, A2

Formerly the private grounds of Palazzo Corsini, Rome's 12-hectare botanical gardens are a little-known, slightly neglected gem and a great place to unwind in a tree-shaded expanse covering the steep slopes of the Gianicolo.

Plants have been cultivated here since the 13th century and the current gardens were established in 1883, when the grounds of Palazzo Corsini were given to the University of Rome. They now contain up to 8000 species, including some of Europe's rarest plants. (Botanical Garden; 06 4991 7107; Largo Cristina di Svezia 24; adult/reduced €8/4; 9am-6.30pm Mon-Sat summer, to 5.30pm winter; Lungotevere della Farnesina, Piazza Trilussa)

Tempietto di Bramante & Chiesa di San Pietro in Montorio CHURCH

5 MAP P164, A3

Considered the first great building of the High Renaissance, Bramante's sublime tempietto (Little Temple; 1508) is a perfect surprise, squeezed into the courtyard of the Chiesa di San Pietro in Montorio, on the spot where St Peter is said to have been crucified. It's small, but perfectly formed; its classically inspired design and ideal proportions epitomise the Renaissance zeitgeist. (06 581 3940; www.sanpietroinmontorio.it; Piazza San Pietro in Montorio 2; chiesa 8.30am-noon & 3-4pm Mon-Fri, tempietto 10am-6pm Tue-Sun; Via Garibaldi)

Gianicolo HILL

6 MAP P164, A4

The verdant hill of Gianicolo (or Janiculum) is dotted by monuments to Giuseppe Garibaldi and his makeshift army, who fought

The view from Gianicolo

pope-backing French troops in one of the fiercest battles in the struggle for Italian unification on this spot in 1849. The Italian hero is commemorated with a massive monument in Piazzale Giuseppe Garibaldi, while his Brazilian-born wife, Anita, has her own monument about 200m away in Piazzale Anita Garibaldi; she died from malaria, together with their unborn child, shortly after the siege. (Passeggiata del Gianicolo, 115, 870)

Eating

Fior di Luna

GELATO €

For many Romans this busy little hub makes the best handmade gelato and sorbet in the world. It's produced in small batches using natural, seasonal ingredients. Seasonal favourites include pear and banana, blueberry yoghurt, strawberry and pistachio (the nuts are ground by hand). Get a kick with a cup of *cafe bio* (organic coffee, €1). Note the 'no franchising' sign. (06 6456 1314; http://fiordiluna.com; Via della Lungaretta 96; gelato from €2.50; 1-8pm Sun & Mon, 1-11pm Tue-Sat; Belli, Viale di Trastevere)

Supplì

ITALIAN €

This blink-and-you-miss-it Trastevere *tavola calda* (hot table) has Roman street food down to an art. Locals queue for its namesake *supplì:* fried risotto balls spiked with *ragù* (meat and tomato sauce) and mozzarella. The family-run eatery also gets top marks for pizza by the slice. Daily specials include gnocchi (Thursday) and fried fish and calamari (Tuesday and Friday). (06 589 71 10; www.suppliroma.it; Via di San Francesco a Ripa 137; pizza & fritti €2.50-6; 9am-10pm Mon-Sat; Viale di Trastevere)

La Renella

BAKERY €

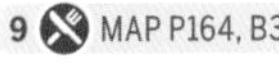

Watch pizza masters at work at this historic Trastevere bakery. Savour the wood-fired ovens, bar-stool seating and heavenly aromas of pizza, bread (get the *casareccia*, crusty Roman-style bread) and biscuits. Piled-high toppings (and

Gianicolo Cannon

If you're meandering through Trastevere, or further afield, and hear a loud crack, panic not, it's just the midday cannon salute from the top of the Gianicolo. In 1847 Pope Pius IX ordered that a cannon fire blank shells at this time daily to set a standard for all the city's bells. Since 1904 it's been shot from the Gianicolo, as it's a little less disturbing from there, but it can still be heard across the city. It wasn't fired during the World Wars, but recommenced in 1959.

Refreshing Grattachecca

It's summertime, the living is easy, and Romans like nothing better in the sultry evening heat than to amble down to the river and partake of some *grattachecca* (crushed ice covered in fruit and syrup). It's the ideal way to cool down, and there are kiosks along the riverbank satisfying this very Roman need; try **Sora Mirella Caffè** (Map p164, D3; Lungotevere degli Anguillara; treats €3-6; 11am-3am May-Sep; Lungotevere degli Anguillara), next to Ponte Cestio. Down by the water, shaved ice in hand, meander north along the river to **Ponte Sisto** and watch the marauding seagulls.

fillings) vary seasonally, to the joy of everyone from punks with big dogs to old ladies with little dogs. It's been in the biz since 1870. (06 581 72 65; http://larenella.com; Via del Moro 15; pizza slices from €2.50; 7am-midnight Sun-Thu, to 3am Fri & Sat; Piazza Trilussa)

Da Enzo

TRATTORIA €€

10 MAP P164, D4

Vintage ochre walls, yellow-checked tablecloths and a traditional menu featuring all the Roman classics: what makes this tiny and staunchly traditional trattoria exceptional is its careful sourcing of local, quality products, many from nearby farms in Lazio. The seasonal, deep-fried Jewish artichokes and the *pasta cacio e pepe* (cheese-and-black-pepper pasta) are among the best in Rome. (06 581 22 60; www.daenzoal29.com; Via dei Vascellari 29; meals €30-35; 12.30-3pm & 7.30-11pm Mon-Sat; Lungotevere Ripa, Belli)

Trattoria Da Teo

TRATTORIA €€

11  MAP P164, D4

One of Rome's classic trattorias, Da Teo buzzes with locals digging into steaming platefuls of Roman standards, such as carbonara, *pasta cacio e pepe* (cheese-and-black-pepper pasta) and the most fabulous seasonal artichokes – both Jewish (deep-fried) and Roman-style (stuffed with parsley and garlic, and boiled). In keeping with hardcore trattoria tradition, Teo's homemade gnocchi is only served on Thursday. Reservations essential. (06 581 83 55; www.facebook.com/Trattoria.da.teo; Piazza dei Ponziani 7; meals €35-45; 12.30-3pm & 7.30-11.30pm Mon-Sat; Viale di Trastevere, Belli)

Zia Restaurant

FUSION €€€

12  MAP P164, A4

After cutting his teeth in the kitchens of a few of the culinary world's most reputable names (Georges Blanc and Gordon Ramsay, for example), up-and-coming chef Antonio Ziantoni forges out on his own with solo venture Zia. The menu exquisitely mates Italian and French cuisine. Look for creative takes on old standards like risotto with baby clams, and cod and potatoes. (06 2348 8093; www.ziarestaurant.com; Via Goffredo Mameli 45; meals €30-50; 12.30-3pm & 7.30-10.30pm Mon-Sat; ; Trastevere/Min P Istruzione)

Drinking

Terra Satis CAFE, WINE BAR

13 MAP P164, D4

This hip neighbourhood cafe and wine bar in Trastevere has it all: newspapers, great coffee and charming bar staff, not to mention vintage furniture, comfy banquette seating and really good snacks. On warm days the laid-back action spills out onto its bijou, vine-covered terrace on cobbled Piazza di Ponziani. Good wine and beer selection. (06 9893 6909; Piazza dei Ponziani 1a; 7am-1am Mon-Thu, to 2am Fri & Sat; ; Viale di Trastevere, Belli)

Bar San Calisto CAFE

14 MAP P164, B3

Head to 'Sanca' for its basic, stuck-in-time atmosphere, cheap prices and large terrace. It attracts everyone from intellectuals to people-watching idlers and foreign students. It's famous for its chocolate – come for hot chocolate with cream in winter, and chocolate gelato in summer. Try the *sambuca con la mosca* ('with flies' – raw coffee beans). Expect occasional late-night jam sessions. (Piazza San Calisto 3-5; 6am-2am Mon-Sat; Viale di Trastevere, Viale di Trastevere)

Rivendita Libri, Cioccolata e Vino COCKTAIL BAR

15 MAP P164, B3

Think of this as Ground Zero of Rome's recent crackdown on debauched drinking. The drinks of a million hen parties – French Kiss, Orgasm and One Night Stand – highlight the cocktail list. The bar is packed every night from around 10pm with a squealing, drinking-pounding crowd. Some cocktails are served in miniature chocolate cups topped with whipped cream. (06 5830 1868; www.facebook.com/cioccolateriatrastevere; Vicolo del Cinque 11a; 6.30pm-2am Mon-Fri, 2pm-2am Sat & Sun; Piazza Trilussa)

Keyhole COCKTAIL BAR

16 MAP P164, B3

This achingly hip, underground speakeasy ticks all the boxes: no identifiable name or signage outside; a black door smothered in keyhole plates; and Prohibition-era decor including Chesterfield sofas, dim lighting and a craft cocktail menu. Not sure what to order? The mixologists will create your own bespoke cocktail (around €10). (Via dell'Arco di San Calisto 17; midnight-5am; Viale di Trastevere, Belli)

Ma Che Siete Venuti a Fà PUB

17 MAP P164, B2

Named after a football chant, which translates politely as 'What did you come here for?', this pint-sized Trastevere pub is a beer-buff's paradise, packing in around 15 international craft beers on tap and even more by the bottle. Although it could easily be a cliche, the vibe here is real, and every surface is covered in beer labels. (☎06 6456 2046; www.football-pub.com; Via Benedetta 25; ⏰11am-2am; 🚌Piazza Trilussa)

Il Baretto BAR

18 MAP P164, A4

Venture up a steep flight of steps from Trastevere – go on, it's worth it. Because here you'll discover this good-looking cocktail bar where the bass lines are meaty, the bar staff hip, and the interior a mix of vintage and pop art. Better yet, stop here on your way *down* from Gianicolo and have something cold on the tree-shaded terrace. (☎06 589 60 55; Via Garibaldi 27; ⏰7am-2am; 🚌Via Garibaldi)

Entertainment

Lettere Caffè LIVE MUSIC

19 MAP P164, C5

Like books? Poetry? Blues and jazz? Then you'll love this place: a clutter of bar stools and books, where there are regular live gigs, poetry slams, comedy and gay nights, plus DJ sets playing electronic, indie and new wave. *Aperitivo*, with a tempting vegetarian buffet, is served between 7pm and 9pm. Enjoy one of the cheap cocktail specials under the whirling fans. (☎340 0044154; www.letterecaffe.org; Via di San Francesco a Ripa 100/101; ⏰6pm-2am, closed mid-Aug–mid-Sep; 🚌Viale di Trastevere, 🚋Trastevere/Mastai)

Shopping

Antica Caciara Trasteverina FOOD & DRINKS

20 MAP P164, B4

The fresh ricotta is a prized possession at this century-old deli, and it's usually gone by lunchtime. If you're too late, take solace in the luscious *ricotta infornata* (oven-baked ricotta), wheels of famous,

Mercato di Porta Portese

SUN_SHINE / SHUTTERSTOCK ©

black-waxed *pecorino romano*, and garlands of *guanciale* (pig's jowl) ready for the perfect carbonara. The lovely, caring staff answer questions and plastic-wrap cheese and hams for transport home. (06 581 28 15; www.facebook.com/anticacaciaratrasteverina; Via di San Francesco a Ripa 140; 7.30am-8pm Mon-Sat; Viale di Trastevere, Trastevere/Mastai)

Biscottificio Innocenti FOOD

21 MAP P164, D4

For homemade biscuits, bite-sized meringues and fruit tarts large and small, there is no finer address in Rome than this vintage *biscottificio* with ceramic-tiled interior, fly-net door curtain and a set of old-fashioned scales on the counter to weigh biscuits (€17 to €25 per kilo). The shop has been run with much love and passion for several decades by the ever-dedicated Stefania. (06 580 39 26; www.facebook.com/biscottificio Innocenti; Via della Luce 21; 8am-8pm Mon-Sat, 9.30am-2pm Sun; Viale di Trastevere, Belli)

Atelier Livia Risi CLOTHING

22 MAP P164, D4

Designer Livia Risi designs women's clothes for that elusive sweet spot: elegant daily wear that's super-comfortable to wear while being both stylish and adaptable. Her wares hang on simple racks in her shop. Buy something ready made or work with her on a creation just for you. (06 5830 1667; www.liviarisi.it; Via dei Vascellari 37; 10.30am-8pm Mon-Sat; Belli)

Porta Portese Market

Head to the mammoth **Mercato di Porta Portese** (Map p164, C6; Piazza Porta Portese; 6am-2pm Sun; Viale di Trastevere, Trastevere/Min P Istruzione) flea market to see Rome bargain-hunting. Thousands of stalls sell everything from rare books and fell-off-a-lorry bikes to Peruvian shawls and off-brand phones. It's crazily busy and a lot of fun. Keep your valuables safe and wear your haggling hat for the inevitable discovery of a treasure amid the dreck.

Les Vignerons WINE

23 MAP P164, A4

If you're looking for interesting vintages, search out this lovely Trastevere wine shop. It boasts one of the capital's best collections of natural wines, mainly from small Italian and French producers, as well as a comprehensive selection of spirits and international craft beers. Staff offer great advice. (06 6477 1439; www.lesvignerons.it; Via Mameli 61; 4-9pm Mon, 11am-9pm Tue-Thu, to 9.30pm Fri & Sat; Viale di Trastevere, Trastevere/Min P Istruzione)

2

Survival Guide

Vespa JAROSLAW PAWLAK / SHUTTERSTOCK ©

Before You Go

Book Your Stay

- Rome is expensive and busy; book your accommodation ahead to secure the best deal.
- Accommodation options range from palatial five-star hotels to hostels, B&Bs, *pensioni* and private rooms; there's also a growing number of boutique suite and apartment hotels.
- Everyone overnighting in Rome pays the *tassa di soggiorno*, a room-occupancy tax on top of their bill: €3 per person per night in one- and two-star hotels; €3.50 in B&Bs and room rentals; €4/6/7 in three-/four-/five-star hotels.
- When you check into your accommodation, you'll need to present your passport or identification card.

Useful Websites

Bed & Breakfast Italia (www.bbitalia.it) Italian bed-and-breakfast network listing many options located throughout Rome.

Cross Pollinate (www.cross-pollinate.com) Personally vetted rooms and apartments by the team that is behind Rome's **Beehive** (www.the-beehive.com) hostel.

Italy Perfect (www.italyperfect.com) Plenty of Rome apartment rentals.

Lonely Planet (www.lonelyplanet.com/italy/rome/hotels) Author-reviewed accommodation options.

Rome Accommodation.net (www.rome-accommodation.net) Apartment and vacation-home rental network.

Rome As You Feel (www.romeasyoufeel.com) Apartment rentals: ranging from studio flats to luxury apartments.

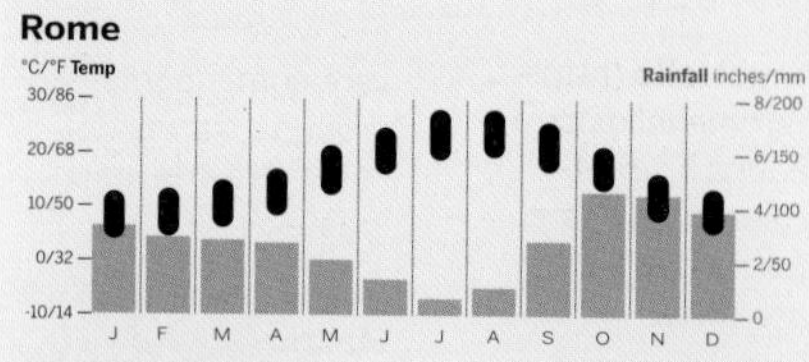

When to Go

- **Winter (Dec–Feb)** Cold, short days. Museums are quiet and prices are low except at Christmas and New Year.
- **Spring (Mar–May)** Warm, sunny weather. Fervent Easter celebrations and azaleas on the Spanish Steps. Busy, with high prices.
- **Summer (Jun–Aug)** Very hot. Plenty of outdoor events. In August, Romans desert the city and hoteliers drop prices.
- **Autumn (Sep–Nov)** Popular period. Warm weather, high prices and the Romaeuropa festival. November brings rain and low-season prices.

Best Budget

RomeHello (https://theromehello.com) Fabulous street-art-adorned hostel operated as a social enterprise.

Althea Inn Roof Terrace (www.altheainnroofterrace.com) Designer comfort at budget prices.

Beehive (www.the-beehive.com) Sustainable, friendly and stylish hostel near Termini.

Hotel San Pietrino (www.sanpietrino.it) Family-run *pensione* within easy walking distance of the Vatican.

Best Midrange

Residenza Maritti (www.residenzamaritti.com) Hidden treasure with captivating views over the Forums.

Arco del Lauro (www.arcodellauro.it) B&B bolthole with ultra-friendly hosts.

66 Imperial Inn (www.66imperialinn.com) Bright and comfortable rooms with plenty of extras.

Relais Le Clarisse (www.leclarissetrastevere.com) Rooms around a tranquil courtyard in bustling Trastevere.

Casa Fabbrini: Campo Marzio (https://campomarzio.casafabbrini.it) Style on a budget in upmarket Tridente.

Best Top End

Villa Spalletti Trivelli (www.villaspalletti.it) Stately style in a city-centre mansion.

Eitch Borromini (www.eitchborromini.com) Elegant rooms and two roof terraces overlooking Piazza Navona.

Argentina Residenza Style Hotel (www.argentinaresidenzastylehotel.com) Charming boutique choice occupying a former monastery.

Palazzo Scanderbeg (www.palazzoscanderbeg.com) Sleek contemporary suites in a 15th-century *palazzo*.

Fendi Private Suites (www.fendiprivatesuites.com) Live the fashion-designer dream inside Palazzo Fendi.

Arriving in Rome

Leonardo da Vinci Airport (Fiumicino)

Rome's main international airport, **Leonardo da Vinci** (☎06 6 59 51; www.adr.it/fiumicino), is 30km west of the city. It currently has two operational terminals, T1 and T3, both within walking distance of each other.

The easiest way to get into town is by train, but there are also buses and private shuttle services.

Leonardo Express Train (www.trenitalia.com; 1 way €14) Runs to/from Stazione Termini. Departures from the airport every 30 minutes between 6.08am and 11.23pm, and from Termini between 5.20am and 10.35pm. Journey time is approximately 30 minutes.

FL1 Train (www.trenitalia.com; 1 way €8) Connects to Trastevere, Ostiense and Tiburtina stations, but not Termini. Departures from the airport every 15 minutes (half-hourly on Sunday and public holidays) between 5.57am and 10.42pm; from Tiburtina every 15 to 30 minutes between 5.01am and 10.01pm.

SIT Bus (☎ 06 591 68 26; www.sitbusshuttle.com; 1 way/return €6/11) Regular departures to Stazione Termini (Via Marsala) from 7.15am to 12.40am; from Termini between 4.45am and 8.30pm. All buses stop near the Vatican (Via Crescenzio 2) en route. Tickets are available on the bus. Journey time is approximately one hour.

Cotral Bus (☎ 800 174471, from a mobile 06 7205 7205; www.cotralspa.it; 1 way €5, purchased on bus €7) Runs between Fiumicino and Stazione Tiburtina via Termini. Four to six daily departures including night services from the airport at 1.45am, 3.45am, and 5.45am, and from Tiburtina at 12.30am, 2.30am and 4.30am. Journey time is one hour.

Schiaffini Rome Airport Bus (☎ 06 713 05 31; www.romeairportbus.com; Via Giolitti; 1 way/return €6.90/9.90) Regular services from the airport to Stazione Termini (Via Giolitti) between 6.05am and midnight; from Termini between 5.10am and 1am. Allow about an hour for the journey.

TAM Bus (☎ 06 6504 74 26; www.tambus.it) Runs buses from the airport to Via Giolitti outside Stazione Termini at least hourly between 12.15am and 11.30pm; to the airport between 12.30am and 11.30pm. Reckon on 40 minutes to one hour journey time.

Airport Connection Services (☎ 338 9876465; www.airportconnection.it) Transfers to/from the city centre start at €22 per person (€28 for two).

Airport Shuttle (☎ 06 4201 3469; www.airportshuttle.it) Transfers to/from your hotel for €25 for one person, then €6 for each additional passenger up to a maximum of eight.

Taxi The set fare to/from the city centre is €48, which is valid for up to four passengers including luggage. Note that taxis registered in Fiumicino charge more, so make sure you catch a Comune di Roma taxi – these are white with a taxi sign on the roof and Roma Capitale written on the door along with the taxi's licence number. Journey time is approximately 45 to 60 minutes depending on traffic.

Ciampino Airport

Ciampino (☎ 06 6 59 51; www.adr.it/ciampino), 15km southeast of the city centre, is used by Ryanair (www.ryanair.com) for European and Italian destinations. It's not a big airport, but there's a steady flow of traffic, and at peak times it gets extremely busy.

To get into town, the best option is to take one of the dedicated bus services. Alternatively, you can take a bus to Ciampino station and then pick up a train to Termini or get a bus to Anagnina metro station (on line A).

Schiaffini Rome Airport Bus (☎ 06 713 05 31; www.romeairportbus.com; Via Giolitti; 1 way/return €5.90/9.90) Regular departures to/from Via Giolitti outside Stazione Termini. From the airport, services are between 4am and 11.45pm; from Via Giolitti, between 4.20am and midnight. Buy tickets on board, online, at the airport or at the bus stop. Journey time is approximately 40 minutes.

SIT Bus (☎06 591 68 26; www.sitbusshuttle.com; to/from airport €6/5, return €9) Regular departures from the airport to Stazione Termini (Via Marsala) between 7.45am and 12.15am; from Termini between 4.30am and 9.30pm. Get tickets online, on the bus or at the desk at Ciampino. Journey time is 45 minutes.

Terravision (www.terravision.eu) Runs from the airport to Stazione Termini between 8.15am and 12.15am; from Termini between 4.30am and 9.20pm. Bank on 45 minutes for the journey.

Atral (www.atral-lazio.com) Runs regular buses between the airport and Anagnina metro station (€1.20) and Ciampino train station (€1.20), from which you can get a train to Termini (€1.50).

Airport Connection Services (☎338 9876465; www.airportconnection.it) Transfers to/from the city centre start at €22 per person (€28 for two).

Airport Shuttle (☎06 4201 3469; www.airportshuttle.it) Transfers to/from your hotel for €25 for one person, then €6 for each additional passenger up to a maximum of eight.

Taxi The set rate to/from the airport is €30. Journey time is approximately 30 minutes depending on traffic.

Stazione Termini & Bus Station

- Rome's main station and principal transport hub is **Stazione Termini** (www.romatermini.com; Piazza dei Cinquecento; M Termini). It has regular connections to other European countries, all major Italian cities and many smaller towns.
- Train information is available from the Customer Service area on the main concourse to the left of the ticket desks. Alternatively, check www.trenitalia.com or phone ☎89 20 21.
- From Termini, you can connect with the metro or take a bus from Piazza dei Cinquecento out front. Taxis are outside the main entrance/exit.
- **Left Luggage** (Stazione Termini; 1st 5hr €6, 6-12hr per hour €1, 13hr & over per hour €0.50; ⏰6am-11pm; M Termini) is available by platform 24 on the Via Giolitti side of the station.

Getting Around

Public transport includes buses, trams, metro and a suburban train network. The main hub is Stazione Termini. Tickets, which come in various forms, are valid for all forms of transport. Children under 10 travel free.

Metro

- Rome has two main metro lines, A (orange) and B (blue), which cross at Termini. A branch line, 'B1', serves the northern suburbs, while work continues on a third line C, which currently runs through the southeastern outskirts from San Giovanni. However, you're unlikely to need these two lines.

- Trains run from 5.30am to 11.30pm (to 1.30am on Friday and Saturday).
- Take line A for the Trevi Fountain (Barberini), Spanish Steps (Spagna) and St Peter's (Ottaviano–San Pietro).
- Take line B for the Colosseum (Colosseo).

Bus

- Rome's public bus service is run by **ATAC** (www.atac.roma.it).
- The **main bus station** (Piazza dei Cinquecento) is in front of Stazione Termini on Piazza dei Cinquecento, where there's an **information booth** (8am-8pm).
- Other important hubs are at Largo di Torre Argentina and Piazza Venezia.
- Buses run from about 5.30am until midnight, with limited services throughout the night.
- Rome's night bus service comprises more than 25 lines, many of which pass Termini and/or Piazza Venezia. Buses are marked with an 'n' before the number and bus stops have a blue owl symbol. Departures are usually every 15 to 30 minutes, but can be much slower.

For route planning and real time information, Roma Bus is a useful phone app.

Tickets & Passes

Public-transport tickets are valid on all buses, trams and metro lines, except for routes to Fiumicino airport.

BIT (a single ticket valid for 100 minutes; in that time it can be used on all forms of transport but only once on the metro) €1.50

Roma 24h (24 hours) €7

Roma 48h (48 hours) €12.50

Roma 72h (72 hours) €18

CIS (weekly ticket) €24

Abbonamento mensile (a monthly pass) for a single user €35

Children under 10 travel free.

Buy tickets from *tabacchi*, newsstands and machines at main bus stops and metro stations. Validate in machines on buses, at metro entrance gates or at train stations. Ticketless riders risk a fine of at least €50.

The Roma Pass (48/72 hours €28/38.50) comes with a travel pass valid within the city boundaries.

Tram

Rome has a limited tram network. For route maps see www.atac.roma.it.

The most useful lines:

- **2** Piazzale Flaminio to/from Piazza Mancini.
- **3** Museo Nazionale Etrusco di Villa Giulia to/from San Lorenzo, San Giovanni, Testaccio and Trastevere.
- **8** Piazza Venezia to/from Trastevere.
- **19** Piazza del Risorgimento to/from Villa Borghese, San Lorenzo, Via Prenestina.

Taxi

- Official licensed taxis are white with a taxi sign on the roof and Roma Capitale written on the front door along with the licence number.
- Always go with the metered fare, never an arranged price (the set fares to/from the airports are exceptions).
- Official rates are posted in taxis and at https://romamobilita.it/it/media/muoversia roma/muoversi-taxi.
- You can hail a taxi, but it's often easier to wait at a rank or phone for one. There are taxi ranks at the airports, Stazione Termini, Piazza della Repubblica, Piazza Barberini, Piazza di Spagna, Piazza Venezia, the Pantheon, the Colosseum, Largo di Torre Argentina, Piazza Belli, Piazza Pio XII, Piazza del Risorgimento.
- To book a taxi, call the automated **taxi line** (in Italian 06 06 09) or use the ChiamaTaxi app.
- MyTaxi is another good app. It allows you to order a taxi without having to deal with tricky language problems.

Buses from Termini

From Piazza dei Cinquecento, outside Stazione Termini, buses run to all corners of the city.

Destination	Bus No
Campo de' Fiori	40/64
Colosseum	75
Pantheon	40/64
Piazza Navona	40/64
Piazza Venezia	40/64
St Peter's Square	40/64
Terme di Caracalla	714
Trastevere	H
Villa Borghese	910

Essential Information

Accessible Travel

- Cobbled streets and tiny lifts are difficult for wheelchair users, while the relentless traffic can be disorienting for partially sighted travellers or those with hearing difficulties.
- If you have an obvious disability and/or appropriate ID, many museums and galleries offer free admission for yourself and a companion.
- To reach the city from Fiumicino, the wheelchair-accessible Leonardo Express train runs to Stazione Termini. Alternatively, **Fausta Trasporti** (06 540 33 62; http://accessibletransportationrome.com) is one of a number of operators offering transfers in wheelchair-accessible vehicles.
- If travelling by train, ring 800 90 60 60 to arrange assistance. At Stazione Termini, the **Sala Blu Assistenza Disabili** (800 90 60 60; SalaBlu.ROMA@rfi.it; 6.45am-9.30pm; M Termini) next to platform 1 can provide information on wheelchair-accessible

trains and help with transport in the station. Contact the office 24 hours ahead if you know you're going to need assistance. There are similar offices at Tiburtina and Ostiense stations.

- All stations on metro line B have wheelchair access and lifts except Circo Massimo, Colosseo and Cavour. On line A, Cipro and Termini are equipped with lifts.
- Bus 590 covers the same route as metro line A and is one of 22 bus and tram services with wheelchair access. Routes with disabled access are indicated on bus stops.
- Some taxis are equipped to carry passengers in wheelchairs; ask for a taxi for a *sedia a rotelle* (wheelchair). **Fausta Trasporti** (http://accessibletransportationrome.com) has a fleet of wheelchair-accessible vehicles that can carry up to seven people, including three wheelchair users.
- Download Lonely Planet's free Accessible Travel guides from http://lptravel.to/AccessibleTravel.

Business Hours

Banks 8.30am–1.30pm and 2.45pm–4.30pm Monday to Friday

Bars & cafes 7.30am–8pm, sometimes until 1am or 2am

Clubs 10pm–4am or 5am

Restaurants noon–3pm and 7.30pm–11pm (later in summer)

Shops 10am–7.30pm or 8pm Monday to Saturday, some also 11am–7pm Sunday; smaller shops 10am–1.30pm and 3.30pm–7.30pm Monday to Saturday; some shops are closed Monday morning

Electricity

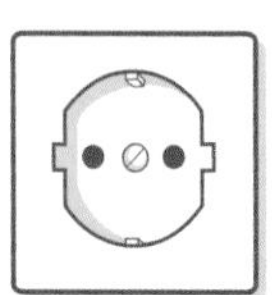

Type F
230V/50Hz

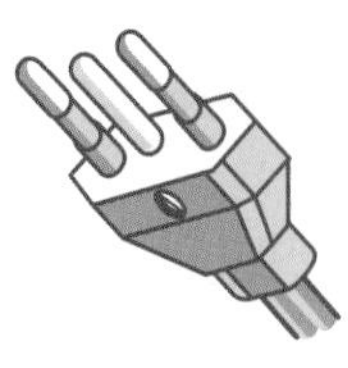

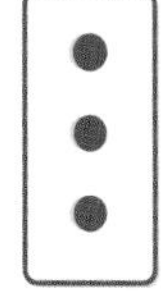

Type L
220V/50Hz

Money

ATMs

- ATMs (known in Italy as *bancomat*) are widely available in Rome, and most will accept cards tied into the Visa, MasterCard, Cirrus and Maestro systems.
- Most ATMs have a daily withdrawal limit of €250.
- Always let your bank know when you're going abroad to prevent your card being frozen when payments from unusual locations appear.

Credit Cards

- Virtually all midrange and top-end hotels

accept credit cards, as do most restaurants and large shops. Some cheaper *pensioni* (pensions), trattorias and pizzerias only accept cash. Don't rely on credit cards at smaller museums or galleries.

- Major cards such as Visa, MasterCard, Eurocard, Cirrus and Eurocheques are widely accepted. Amex is also recognised, although it's less common than Visa or MasterCard.

Discount Cards

Omnia Card (adult/reduced €113/80; valid for 72 hours) Includes fast-track entry to the Vatican Museums and admission to St Peter's Basilica, Basilica di San Giovanni in Laterano and Carcere Mamertino. It allows free travel on hop-on hop-off Open Bus Vatican & Rome, plus unlimited public transport within Rome. Entry is free to two sites, with a 50% discount to extra sites. A 24-hour version is also available (€55). Details at www.omniakit.org.

Roma Pass (€38.50; valid for 72 hours) Includes free admission to two museums or sites, as well as reduced entry to extra sites, unlimited city transport & discounted entry to other exhibitions & events. The 48-hour Roma Pass (€28) is a more limited version. Details at www.romapass.it.

Tipping

Romans are not big tippers, but the following is a rough guide:

Bars Not necessary, although many people leave small change if drinking at the bar.

Hotels Tip porters about €5 at A-list hotels.

Restaurants Service *(servizio)* is generally included; if it's not, a euro or two is fine in pizzerias and trattorias, no more than five to 10% in smart restaurants.

Taxis Optional, but most people round up to the nearest euro.

Public Holidays

Most Romans take their annual holidays in August. This means that many businesses and shops close for at least part of the month, particularly around Ferragosto (Feast of the Assumption) on 15 August.

Public holidays in Rome include the following:

Capodanno (New Year's Day) 1 January

Epifania (Epiphany) 6 January

Pasquetta (Easter Monday) March/April

Giorno Liberazione (Liberation Day) 25 April

Festa del Lavoro (Labour Day) 1 May

Festa della Repubblica (Republic Day) 2 June

Festa dei Santi Pietro e Paolo (Feast of Saints Peter and Paul) 29 June

Ferragosto (Feast of the Assumption) 15 August

Festa di Ognisanti (All Saints' Day) 1 November

Festa dell'Immacolata Concezione (Feast of

the Immaculate Conception) 8 December

Natale (Christmas Day) 25 December

Festa di Santo Stefano (Boxing Day) 26 December

Responsible Travel

Covid Protocols

- Masks must be worn in indoor public places and on public transport.
- A Green Pass (vaccination certificate) is required for indoor dining at restaurants and to access museums.
- Check the latest regulations at www.italia.it/en/useful-info/covid-19-updates-information-for-tourists.html.

Overtourism

- Avoid crowds by visiting off-season, between November and March.
- Consider staying in less-central neighbourhoods such as Testaccio, Aventino, Prati, or San Giovanni.

Safe Travel

Rome is a safe city, but petty theft can be a problem. Use common sense and watch your valuables.

- Pickpockets and thieves are active in touristy areas such as the Colosseum, Piazza di Spagna, Piazza Venezia and St Peter's Square.
- Be alert around Stazione Termini and on crowded public transport – the 64 Vatican bus is notorious.
- In case of theft or loss, always report the incident to the police within 24 hours and ask for a statement.

Telephone Services

- Local SIM cards can be used in European, Australian and unlocked US phones. Other phones must be set to roaming.
- Italian mobile phones operate on the GSM 900/1800 network, which is compatible with the rest of Europe and Australia but not always with the North American GSM or CDMA systems – check with your service provider.
- The cheapest way of using your mobile is to buy a prepaid *(prepagato)* Italian SIM card. TIM (Telecom Italia Mobile; www.tim.it), Wind (www.wind.it), Vodafone (www.vodafone.it) and Tre (www.tre.it) all offer SIM cards and have retail outlets across town.
- Note that by Italian law all SIM cards must be registered in Italy, so make sure you have a passport or ID card with you when you buy one.

Toilets

Public toilets are not widespread, but you'll find them at St Peter's Square (free) and Stazione Termini (€1). If you're caught short, the best thing to do is to nip into a cafe or bar.

Tourist Information

There are tourist information points at **Fiumicino** (Fiumicino Airport; International Arrivals, Terminal 3; 8am-8.45pm) and **Ciampino** (Arrivals Hall; 8.30am-6pm) airports, as well as the following locations across the city:

Castel Sant'Angelo (www.turismoroma.it; Piazza Pia; 9.30am-7pm summer, 8.30am-6pm winter; Piazza Pia)

Imperial Forums (Map p46; Via dei Fori Imperiali; 9.30am-7pm, to 8pm Jul & Aug; Via dei Fori Imperiali)

Pazza delle Cinque Lune (Map p60; Piazza delle Cinque Lune; 9.30am-7pm; Corso del Rinascimento) Near Piazza Navona.

Stazione Termini (06 06 08; www.turismoroma.it; Via Giovanni Giolitti 34; 8am-6.45pm; M Termini) In the hall adjacent to platform 24.

Trastevere (www.turismoroma.it; Piazza Sonnino; 10.30am-8pm; Viale di Trastevere, Belli)

Via Marco Minghetti (06 06 08; www.turismoroma.it; Via Marco Minghetti; 9.30am-7pm; Via del Corso) Between Via del Corso and the Trevi Fountain.

For information about the Vatican, contact the **Ufficio Pellegrini e Turisti** (Map p86, C5; 06 6988 1662; www.vatican.va; St Peter's Sq; 8.30am-6.30pm Mon-Sat; Piazza del Risorgimento, M Ottaviano-San Pietro).

Rome's official tourist website, **Turismo Roma** (www.turismoroma.it), has comprehensive information about sights, accommodation and city transport, as well as itineraries and up-to-date listings.

The **Comune di Roma** (06 06 08; www.060608.it; 9am-7pm) runs a free multilingual tourist information phone line providing info on culture, shows, hotels, transport etc. Its website is also an excellent resource.

Dos & Don'ts

Do...

- Greet people in bars, shops, trattorias etc with a *buongiorno* (good morning) or *buonasera* (good evening).
- Dress the part – cover up when visiting churches and go smart when eating out.
- Eat pasta with a fork, not a spoon; it's OK to eat pizza with your hands.

Don't...

- Feel you have to order everything on the menu. No one seriously expects you to eat a starter, pasta, second course and dessert.
- Order cappuccino after lunch or dinner. Well OK, you can, but Romans don't.
- Wait for cars to stop at pedestrian crossings. You'll have to make the first move if you want to cross the road.

Visas

- Italy is one of the 26 European countries making up the Schengen area. The visa rules that apply to Italy apply to all Schengen countries.
- EU citizens do not need a visa to enter Italy – a valid ID card or passport is sufficient.
- Nationals of some other countries, including Australia, Canada, Israel, Japan, New Zealand, Switzerland and the USA, do not need a visa for stays of up to 90 days.
- Nationals of other countries will need a Schengen tourist visa – to check requirements see www.schengenvisainfo.com/tourist-schengen-visa.

Language

Regional dialects are an important part of identity in many parts of Italy, but you'll have no trouble being understood in Rome or anywhere else in the country if you stick to standard Italian, which is what we've also used in this chapter.

The sounds used in Italian can all be found in English. If you read our pronunciation guides as if they were English, you'll be understood. The stressed syllables are indicated with italics. Note that *ai* is pronounced as in 'aisle', *ay* as in 'say', *ow* as in 'how', *dz* as the 'ds' in 'lids', and that *r* is a strong and rolled sound.

To enhance your trip with a phrasebook, visit lonelyplanet.com.

Basics

Hello.
Buongiorno. bwon·*jor*·no

Goodbye.
Arrivederci. a·ree·ve·*der*·chee

How are you?
Come sta? *ko*·me sta

Fine. And you?
Bene. E Lei? *be*·ne e lay

Please.
Per favore. per fa·*vo*·re

Thank you.
Grazie. *gra*·tsye

Excuse me.
Mi scusi. mee *skoo*·zee

Sorry.
Mi dispiace. mee dees·*pya*·che

Yes./No.
Sì./No. see/no

I don't understand.
Non capisco. non ka·*pee*·sko

Do you speak English?
Parla inglese? *par*·la een·*gle*·ze

Eating & Drinking

I'd like ...	*Vorrei ...*	vo·*ray* ..
a coffee	*un caffè*	oon ka·*fe*
a table	*un tavolo*	oon *ta*·vo·lo
the menu	*il menù*	eel me·*noo*
two beers	*due birre*	doo·e *bee*·re

What would you recommend?
Cosa mi consiglia? ko·za mee kon·see·lya

Enjoy the meal!
Buon appetito! bwon a·pe·*tee*·to

That was delicious!
Era squisito! e·ra skwee·zee·to

Cheers!
Salute! sa·*loo*·te

Please bring the bill.
Mi porta il conto, per favore? mee *por*·ta eel *kon* to per fa·*vo*·re

Shopping

I'd like to buy ...
Vorrei comprare ... vo·*ray* kom·*pra*·re ...

I'm just looking.
Sto solo guardando. sto *so*·lo gwar·*dan*·do

How much is this?

Quanto costa questo?	kwan·to kos·ta kwe·sto

It's too expensive.

È troppo caro/ cara. (m/f)	e tro·po ka·ro/ ka·ra

Emergencies

Help!

Aiuto!	a·yoo·to

Call the police!

Chiami la polizia!	kya·mee la po·lee·tsee·a

Call a doctor!

Chiami un medico!	kya·mee oon me·dee·ko

I'm sick.

Mi sento male.	mee sen·to ma·le

I'm lost.

Mi sono perso/ persa. (m/f)	mee so·no per·so/ per·sa

Where are the toilets?

Dove sono i gabinetti?	do·ve so·no ee ga·bee·ne·tee

Time & Numbers

What time is it?

Che ora è?	ke o·ra e

It's (two) o'clock.

Sono le (due).	so·no le (doo·e)

morning	*mattina*	ma·tee·na
afternoon	*pomeriggio*	po·me·ree·jo
evening	*sera*	se·ra
yesterday	*ieri*	ye·ree
today	*oggi*	o·jee
tomorrow	*domani*	do·ma·nee

1	*uno*	oo·no
2	*due*	doo·e
3	*tre*	tre
4	*quattro*	kwa·tro
5	*cinque*	cheen·kwe
6	*sei*	say
7	*sette*	se·te
8	*otto*	o·to
9	*nove*	no·ve
10	*dieci*	dye·chee
100	*cento*	chen·to
1000	*mille*	mee·le

Transport & Directions

Where's ...?

Dov'è ...?	do·ve ...

What's the address?

Qual'è l'indirizzo?	kwa·le leen·dee·ree·tso

Can you show me (on the map)?

Può mostrarmi (sulla pianta)?	pwo mos·trar·mee (soo·la pyan·ta)

At what time does the ... leave?

A che ora parte ...?	a ke o·ra par·te

Does it stop at ...?

Si ferma a ...?	see fer·ma a ...

How do I get there?

Come ci si arriva?	ko·me chee see a·ree·va

bus	*l'autobus*	low·to·boos
ticket	*un biglietto*	oon bee·lye·to
timetable	*orario*	o·ra·ryo
train	*il treno*	eel tre·no

Behind the Scenes

Send Us Your Feedback

We love to hear from travellers – your comments help make our books better. We read every word, and we guarantee that your feedback goes straight to the authors. Visit **lonelyplanet.com/contact** to submit your updates and suggestions.

Note: We may edit, reproduce and incorporate your comments in Lonely Planet products such as guidebooks, websites and digital products, so let us know if you don't want your comments reproduced or your name acknowledged. For a copy of our privacy policy visit lonelyplanet.com/privacy.

Duncan's Thanks

A big thank you to fellow authors Virginia Maxwell and Alexis Averbuck for their suggestions and to Anna Tyler at Lonely Planet for all her support. In Rome *grazie* to Alexandra Bruzzese for her foodie tips and Richard McKenna for his ever-entertaining lunch company. As always, a big, heartfelt hug to Lidia and the boys, Ben and Nick.

Acknowledgements

Cover photograph: Roman Forum, Viacheslav Lopatin/Shutterstock ©

This Book

This 7th edition of Lonely Planet's *Pocket Rome* guidebook was researched and written by Duncan Garwood, Alexis Averbuck and Virginia Maxwell. The previous edition was written by the same authors. This guidebook was produced by the following:

Destination Editor Anna Tyler

Senior Product Editors Daniel Bolger, Elizabeth Jones

Product Editors Will Allen, Kate James, Alison Ridgway

Book Designers Hannah Blackie, Wibowo Rusli

Assisting Editors Ronan Abayawickrema, Bruce Evans, Emma Gibbs, Jennifer Hattam, Alison Morris, Sarah Stewart, Simon Williamson

Cartographers Hunor Csutoros, Julie Dodkins, Anthony Phelan

Cover Researcher Hannah Blackie

Thanks to Alison Anderstrem, Alexandra Bruzzese, Nicki Curry, Gemma Graham, Martin Heng, Brian Taylor, Joy Virden, Brana Vladisavljevic

Index

See also separate subindexes for:

Eating p189
Drinking p190
Entertainment p190
Shopping p190

Sights 000
Map Pages **000**

Eating

Drinking

Entertainment

Shopping

Sights 000
Map Pages **000**